1989

MY
FIRST SEVENTY
YEARS

By Sister M. Madeleva, C.S.C.

COLLECTED POEMS
AMERICAN TWELFTH NIGHT
AND OTHER POEMS
MY FIRST SEVENTY YEARS

Sister M. Madeleva, C.S.C.

MY
FIRST SEVENTY
YEARS

THE MACMILLAN COMPANY
New York 1959

Nihil obstat:

Edward A. Miller
Censor Librorum

Imprimatur:

✠ Leo A. Pursley
Bishop of Fort Wayne

Third Printing 1959

Library of Congress catalog card number: 59-6135

The Macmillan Company, New York
Brett-Macmillan Ltd., Galt, Ontario

Printed in the United States of America

To
Our School of Sacred Theology
Teachers and Students
God's Gift to Us

For their kindness
in reading my manuscript
and permitting its publication
I wish to thank
Mother Mary Clare, our Provincial
and
Mother Kathryn Marie, our
Superior General

Preface

IT HAS always interested me to observe the variety of titles under which authors expose their lives in print. It would be more interesting to explore further possibilities in this very old and fascinating form of self-revelation. Sister Madeleva has made no attempt to find a clever and "catchy" name for her story. Betraying none of the usual reluctance of ladies to tell their age, she calls it simply, MY FIRST SEVENTY YEARS, implying thereby that there will be more, as indeed there will be. The thoughtful religious mind is never far from the vision and intimation of things beyond mere time. Then, too, nuns do not grow old as other people do. Something in their vocation, their habit and their habits, keeps them young.

This note of youthful vitality, awareness, exhilaration, runs steadily through Sister Madeleva's account of her busy life, so well divided and yet somehow united by the elements that give it its character and its completion: the application of the student and teacher, the absorption of the creative artist, the decisive action of the administrator. She brings to the telling of her story the woman's fine instinct for significant and colorful detail, the poet's rare sense of beauty and the inner meaning of human experience, what the eye sees, the mind contemplates, the heart embraces.

Here is a record of early midwestern Americana in delightful recollections of childhood and adolescence; a travelogue of journeys and sojourns abroad in which the author's own rich cultural background invests every scene with its authentic charm and makes the reader feel that he, too, is there; a catalogue of arresting names in contemporary literature known and admired perceptively for their work, but presented as "people" with a familiar touch that gives us a taste of their quality; adventures into new fields of learning which called for a strong, independent mind, an enterprising spirit and no small degree of perseverance; reflections on education in general and observations on the education of women in particular which are sometimes incisive, often penetrating and always sound and constructive.

It is expected that much of Sister Madeleva's book should be concerned with Saint Mary's College, of which she has been an intimate part as student and teacher, in the development of which she has been an important factor, a leading actor, as President through twenty-five years of progress—the kind of progress that is not measured entirely by expanded facilities and increased enrollment, though there are now impressive evidences of both. These chapters will awaken nostalgic memories among thousands of devoted alumnae; but they will interest others no less, if for less personal reasons, simply as the picture of a courageous college struggling against odds to achieve its ideals and moving forward under enlightened leadership toward their fuller realization.

Sister Madeleva is quick to assure us that she has not written here a spiritual treatise. I have no doubt that she could do so. The depth of her own religious life is implicit on every page. At a time when a few nuns have attracted public attention by articulating their personal problems in print, it is refreshing to know well one of the many who meet their adjustment difficulties without any overpowering temptation to "leap over the wall." In the case of Sister Madeleva a great many people are thankful for that.

✠ Leo A. Pursley
Bishop of Fort Wayne

Contents

Dear Readers

You may find this book disappointing. The chronicle of my threescore years and ten is not a story of a nun on her *prie-dieu*. It does not move in an atmosphere of pink and blue devotions. It is quite free from devout aspirations. Aspiration and inspiration may be implicit. I hope that they are.

The life of every religious is set in a well balanced framework, the order of the day. Within such a plan, as constant and regular as the days of the week and the months of the year, I have lived for the past fifty years. My every day from 5:00 or 5:30 in the morning until 9:00 or 10:00 at night has included: morning and evening prayers, meditation, Holy Mass, Office chanted three times a day, spiritual reading, vocal prayers. Monthly and annual retreats have led me into rich spiritual oases. In fifty years you may be sure that regularity in this régime has been realized with varying approaches toward perfection. Imperfection may be a better word. I have not spoken of these. I have given you no assurance that I have tried to be a good Sister of the Holy Cross. The evidence may not even come through on the pages which follow.

What we think and what we feel, particularly in matters of religion and religious experiences, are not synonymous. Our thought we can share freely and happily. We have words for much of what we think. Our profoundest feelings we need not try to explain even to ourselves. They simply are. The silence of my text is all that I can tell you of these.

Given the order of my day, let us go forward with the record of how it and the grace of God have worked in the case of one girl out of hundreds.

I

The Twenty-fourth of May

In 1887, May twenty-fourth was the feast of Our Lady, Help of Christians, in the liturgical calendar. England celebrated it as the birthday of Queen Victoria. Canada called it "Queen's Day." Among the numerous small towns in northwestern Wisconsin is the island city of Cumberland. Here, on this day, I came to town. In the home of August and Lucy Wolff, I had been preceded nineteen months earlier by a brother, Julius Frederick. Our brother, Werner Peter, arrived two and a half years later. I was baptized Mary Evaline.

Twenty-four years before, a young Pomeranian widow with her three children, August, William and Augusta had landed, after a twenty-seven-day sea voyage in a sailing vessel, in New York City. They became a part of a German colony in the environs of Milwaukee, settling finally just west of Watertown. Little August Frederick, aged nine, with the vanished prestige of the Holy Roman Empire reflected in his name, immediately found himself odd jobs as errand boy or the like. Honest, observant, generous, he was self-supporting at the age of eleven. An apprentice of an expert saddler, he became a harness maker, loving and honoring his trade which he discontinued only at the age of ninety. He liked to think of himself as the oldest craftsman in a trade which he used whimsically to say was killed by gasoline.

The Ringlings were a family of harness makers in Baraboo, a city somewhat larger than Watertown and very near it. Here young August worked at the bench with the four Ringling boys. The call of the "Big Top" already stirred the blood of young Johnny, aged fourteen. He ran away. August Wolff, little older nor larger, was sent in pursuit. As you know, he found and brought him home.

Operating the harness shop in the General Store of Isaac Alsbacher in Mauston, Wisconsin, the young craftsman met Lucy Arntz, a teacher during school time, and a summer clerk in the store. Lucy was the third of the thirteen children of Peter and Bernadine Arntz. Her parents had come to the United States from Essen, Germany, in the 1840's. Peter was thirty-five, a linguist, a world traveler, a pioneer; Bernadine, nineteen, delicately reared, educated by tutors. During her first eight months in the wilderness of Wisconsin, she saw no women except Indian squaws. Yet, always even the roughest workmen in the mill or on the farm paid her the spontaneous tribute, "Mrs. Arntz is a lady."

Peter Arntz had come to America at the call of its pioneer forests, its lumber industry. He chose for his millsite what is now head of the Dells on the Wisconsin river. Because of his superior education, he became secretary to the Lieutenant Governor of the then territory of Wisconsin. Many a committee met in the great dining-room-kitchen of the spacious home where now the Arntz Hotel stands.

Frozen almost into helplessness breaking roads through impassable snowdrifts for his men and his horses, Peter was physically unable to develop his lumber business. It may be a matter of interest to some to know that the timber in the first buildings of the Dominican Convent at Sinsinawa, Wisconsin, came from his mill.

Lucy had gentility and pluck in her make-up. When the young harness maker in Mauston proposed homemaking in Cumberland, she accepted life partnership in a quaint idyllic business with the smell of leather on it. Into their home and their business, I was born these seventy-one years ago.

You should know something of our town of fifteen hundred inhabitants. It lay on an island about two miles long, stretching north and south in the blue sandy-shored Beaver Dam Lake. Front or Main Street for business and Back Street for homes make their way with the contour of the island from end to end. Cross streets and lake shores provide school, church, and home sites. The lake extends five miles north. At its head, one can enter a second lake and so on for twenty miles until one comes to a village of Chippewa Indians. Here in my childhood lived old Cutlip and his squaw, Curly Pipe, Jack Wake Me Up, and a family registered in the county school records under the name "Little Bear Roll Down the Hill and Sleep Three Days." Because these Indians brought deer hair and buckskins to my father's shop, they are among my earliest memories and my cherished friends.

The lake is one of the deep loves of my life. I met it first when I was scarcely two years old. The time was Sunday evening and we were going for a boat ride. Standing on the shore and looking at more water in one place than I had ever seen before, I announced decisively, "I don't want to get into that big tub." But my capitulation was complete. Even today my first question about my home town touches the lake: "Is it high or low this year?" and so on.

From the time I could balance myself precariously on skates I was the first girl on and the last girl off the ice in winter. Sometimes a single boy, more daring than myself, had got ahead of me, but I loved the thrill of spinning off with the ice cracking under every stroke.

I learned to swim dog-fashion with a small board under my

chest, and loved to swim across the lake in its narrowest part. Beaver Dam Lake taught me so much of the wonder and beauty of water that years later, at Carmel, California, I rushed into the Pacific for the first time, breathlessly confident that I could hold the entire ocean and it could hold me, each in the other's arms.

II

The Cat Is Black

A SIXTH birthday on May 24, 1893, gave me a certain maturity in entering the first grade of our public and only school in September of that year. This I realized when a worried mother left her son, older, larger, but worlds less independent than myself, in my care. She assured him that he could depend upon me. Naturally, it pleases me to record that for many years now he has been a most successful lawyer in New York City.

In the third seat from the back, second row of the A class, first grade, I immediately began a short course in self-education. Our first lesson in reading, writing, and spelling looked us straight in the face from the blackboard in the front of the room. On the broadly-ruled lines, in perfect Spencerian penmanship, ran the legend, "The cat is black."

My nicely ruled slate in my right hand, my pencil in my left, I began at once to copy, from the *k* right to left, the model on the board. With a feeling of relative assurance that I had already anticipated most of her work for the year in my regard, I presented my slate to our beloved Miss Williams when she reached my place in the room. She looked at it with something less than the unqualified satisfaction that I had expected. Then she said gently, "Yes, but now, dear, suppose we take the pencil

5

in the other hand and begin at the other side of the slate and the other end of the sentence."

The old feud between left hand and right was on again. I had encountered it at the dining table with my small knife and fork and spoon. Now it asserted itself in others of my life's tools, my slate and pencil. The cat is still black, but I must say so with my right hand, traveling horizontally from left to right.

Even now, in hours of sleeplessness, my mind goes back to this first half hour of school. It travels from right to left, following the first pattern of script it ever directed, repeating again and again the lefthanded report "The cat is black" on Eva Wolff's small slate.

Lead pencils succeeded slates in the second grade. Here, during recess, I had my first grapefruit. My chum, Anna, had a brother in the railroad offices of Saint Paul. To this big city of the Northwest came the fabulous fruits of the then promised land of California. Grapefruit was such. Bill had brought some home. Anna and I had one to share. Bill said it was a treat. We believed him. With difficulty we peeled our fruit and divided it equally, section by section. Faith in Bill and experimental knowledge were at odds. Compromise was required. We settled by thanking Bill for our now superior knowledge, admitting to each other that the fruit had not completely fulfilled our dreams. Womanwise, however, we agreed that there might be other ways of eating grapefruit with which we were not acquainted.

Spencerian pens, ink and small inkwells and glossy paper marked the new academic levels of the third grade. Also two bookshelves in the back of the room held juvenile books that we were allowed to take home. *Dolly Dimple Fly Away* and *Toby Tyler or Ten Weeks with a Circus* were my first enchanting withdrawals. The great attic above our dining room and kitchen held stacks of *Homiletic Review,* stored there by our pastor. On rainy Saturdays I used to pore helplessly over them. After my taste had been formed by Dolly Dimple and Toby I wondered if in all my life I could ever read a book without pictures and conversations.

Methods in writing appear to measure these years of elementary education. Vertical writing began to invade the blackboards. My fourth-grade teacher wrote a precise, tailored, vertical hand. It fitted my mind and its demands for simplicity and legibility. My penmanship today is a survival or an evolution of my still loyal imitation of Miss Anderson.

In the seventh and eighth grades I encountered one of the great teachers of my life. Mrs. Kavanaugh, left a widow shortly after the birth of her only child, returned to teaching as a livelihood and a life. No student ever forgot her. We gave her the complete deference of semifearful obedience and unqualified respect. In seventh grade we studied stocks and bonds. In eighth we anticipated the first quarter of high school algebra. These were rewards for having completed the normal grade work better than well. Shakespeare and Latin were other such rewards. We lived to learn, so learning to live richly.

To our seventh-grade physiology class, the doctor in the town brought the human skeleton from his laboratory for us to look at, to handle. It did us good to know that each of us was housing, under our young flesh and blood, such an ivory scaffold. We saw bits of our own scaffolding through his X ray, very new in 1898. The butcher brought us calves' brains, hearts and eyes, lobes, auricles, ventricles, lungs which we held in our childish hands. This laboratory Mrs. Kavanaugh made possible in her seventh- and eighth-grade kingdom, totaling not more than thirty hungry, thirsty subjects.

She procured for us from a school board full of faith and good works the best relief maps of our five major continents that I have ever seen. She saw us standing on the threshold of the twentieth century as makers of it and our places in it. Etymology became, and because of her still is for me, a beloved land of the wonder of words. Mythology still lives. I find myself more at home with Perseus and Jason and the Centaurs than with the headlines of the morning papers. *The Lady of the Lake* was not Scott, but Scotland. Ellen and James Fitz-James and Roderick Dhu are my own eighth-grade classmates, albeit literary celebrities.

June came and graduation from the grades. In September I would take my second big academic step. I would go into high school.

III

Horse and Buggy Days

CUMBERLAND was one of the many small mill towns that mark the ruthless destruction of our primeval forests; sawmills, planing mills, shingle mills edged one end of the lake. Fresh-cut lumber stood in piles like small Rockefeller Centers near them. They formed so much a part of our childhood thinking that during electric storms, after deafening bursts of thunder, we would exclaim, "The lumber piles are falling down!" and run to the window to see. But always they remained perpendicular, new, clean-smelling with fascinating walks for us to run through and play among.

Our shop on Front Street, and our home in a yard occupying a quarter of the block on Back Street, offered unique variety and place for play. My friends, the trees, dominated our entire domain. I had a pact with myself that I had climbed or could climb every one of them except the giant elms. Often, on sunny summer mornings mother would come out to the yard to be greeted by a child's voice calling from the blue, "Mama, find me!" Finally, she would find her small daughter, perched jauntily on a branch at the top of a basswood or a maple tree. There were a thorn apple and one particular maple that still remain mine in the memory of our family.

Swings, hammock, croquet grounds had their proper places. Plum, cherry, apple groves had theirs. There were the perennial shrubs, flower and vegetable gardens, the small fruits, currants, raspberries, strawberries. We each had our own responsibilities for these. Fred was the master berry-picker, Vern the inventor of ways and means. I had charge of the asparagus bed and the strawberry patch. In this world of growing things, we knew and marked the seasons accurately. We watched the continuing mystery of creation.

For many years, hard and soft woods furnished the fuel of the north. Every home had its woodshed. Ours was a large one, so large that one half was filled with double trapezes, rings, bars. Here many a three-pin-admission show took place. Here many a terrified mother watched her offspring twisted into birds' nests or hanging from trapezes by their heels.

No children now, and few at any time, have had a harness shop for a playhouse. We had. The big back room was piled high with empty boxes of all kinds. Goods from the wholesale houses had been shipped in them: everything from buffalo robes to silver mountings for light driving harness. In the early nineties, the largest of these boxes were filled with beautiful, heavy handmade logging harness and shipped to the Weyerhauser Lumber Camps in the state of Washington.

We children learned to use pliers, pincers, hammers in opening boxes, in sorting nails and tacks, in nailing the empty boxes partly shut. We anticipated modern perpendicular architecture in our piled-up box houses. We set up stores and played house in the largest boxes.

The workroom had built-in benches on all the walls: cutting benches, splicing and riveting benches, workbenches. These were provided with fascinating tools and as many stitching horses as they could accommodate. We played among the big rolls of pungent leather. We tangled and untangled knotted rope. When we could pre-empt an idle stitching horse, we hitched it up with a quickly improvised rope harness and drove away into worlds of make-believe.

Eventually, all the handwork in the shop was replaced by machinery. Eventually, the harness trade became a lost trade. For my father, it was always a craft and an art. He loved it. For more than sixty years, the best harness makers in our northwest served their apprenticeship in his shop.

In 1946 I visited my home in Cumberland for the last time. One morning I walked into the shop to find father seated on his stitching horse with a golden-haired little girl of four beside him. He was teaching her to sew on leather with two wax threads and two blunt needles.

The front room was the salesroom: walls hung with harness, collars, hames, shelves piled with sweat pads, racks laden with robes, counters bright with blankets. The whip rack fascinated us. Here we could choose among dozens of whips to see which would crack loudest, most imperatively. On wooden horses we could sit astride great western saddles, or mount elegantly on the women's sidesaddles of the day. Buckles, snaps, red and green tassels, flynets—what a world of unwonted toys! Best of all were the bells: pairs of bells, strings of sleigh bells, cow bells, sheep bells. On the president's table in the dining room of Saint Mary's College today an imported French bell is rung before every meal. This gives the signal for silence before grace. It is a sheep bell from my father's harness shop.

The harness maker at Cumberland automatically enjoyed the use of the best horses and carriages in the livery stables. This meant long drives in the country on summer Sunday afternoons. The three children took turns sitting in the front seat and helping to drive. Going into the country, father and mother told us the names of the grains and vegetables in the fields we passed. Returning, we made the identifications for them. A clump of lovely wildflowers, a patch of bright raspberries or strawberries always brought us to a stop and a minor raid.

Sunday afternoons in winter hold very dear memories for me. Father and I would climb into "our big chair" and read poetry aloud. Father always had a store: the "memory-gem" collections of those days, or better still, his own scrapbooks of poems clipped from newspapers and magazines. These he kept and shared with me until his death.

Both our grandfathers had died before we could have known them. Visiting the homes of our parents meant "going to grandma's." This we did biennially, at least. I was just past three on the first of these visits that I can remember. We stopped overnight in Madison. My younger brother was still a baby, and the maid in the hotel dressed me and took me alone to the dining room. When the family arrived they found me already sitting in state, having ordered my breakfast of strawberries and chicken.

Later in the day, like simple small-town folk we called on Governor Peck. No less simple than his guests he received us graciously and took us through the capitol. We left the baby asleep on the couch in his office. You will understand now why *Peck's Bad Boy* and *Peck's Uncle Ike and the Red-Headed Boy* were classics in our childhood.

One remembers southern Wisconsin in the 1890's for its woods, blue lakes, rollicking rivers, banked in places by wind and water-sculptured bluffs. Grandmother Arntz's farm lay in such a spot at the juncture of the Lemonware with the Wisconsin River. Here we climbed among the rocks, waded the river, slid down haystacks. Here our stalwart young uncles tossed us astride the big farm horses as they led them down to water after work.

On our last visit to the farm, when I was perhaps twelve, mother took me one late afternoon on a walk along the places dear to her childhood. We climbed the highest bluff and looked down at the tumultuous river fifty feet below. But between it and us, sheathed in its single leaf, a showy orchid, a lovely pink moccasin flower lifted its beauty for us to share. To me it was "beauty's self and beauty's giver."

We walked back to the house quietly. As we climbed over a stile leading into the garden, we stopped, moved by the wordless loveliness of the afternoon. As we stood, saying nothing at all, a whippoorwill sang its wistful wonder of that hour, the most complete I have ever shared with my mother.

My father's home stood just at the west city limits of Watertown. Here we saw flax grown, spun, woven into linen for the beds in which we slept. And, in the name of all beauty-rests, we slept between feather beds.

Grandmother's great looms stood in the north half of the upstairs of the big barn. On winter nights at home we used to tear and sew carpet rags, roll them into great balls of assorted colors. The hit-and-miss balls were the biggest. All were sent to grandma. Sitting on the bench beside her, I would watch for hours her busy traffic of shuttled woof among the dexterously threaded warp of the loom. She was weaving our carpet rags into the bright carpets that were to be the floor coverings of our bedrooms.

The smokehouse was an epicure's delight. Sausages of all shapes and varieties, smoked goose breasts, cheeses were among the delicacies ranged there in neat German order. "Going to grandma's" was no commonplace experience.

As we grew older, we visited hop fields and the great sheds in which the hops were cured. We walked through blocks of seasoning cheeses. Father had a quasi theory that ordinary cheese belonged in mousetraps, but Wisconsin cheese was made for men.

Grandfather Arntz and his men had cut the lumber off the main streets of Milwaukee. Naturally, we entered the city in a mood of squatter's rights. In my uncle's crockery store I was allowed to make my own choice of a set of play dishes. I selected a set of Spode ware in pretty red—six of everything, plates big enough for bread and butter service and cups for demitasse. A child's sense of beauty was already stirring in my subconsciousness.

Our horse and buggy days were happy ones. We lived with the mystery of the seasons: the aurora, sundogs, halos round the moon, the first robin, the first hepaticas, the first fresh strawberries, summer rainbows, or flaming autumns.

Let me make a composite of three incidents in summary. The winter of my fourth year mother became precariously ill. Our third little brother was born prematurely and baptized Leo for our then reigning pontiff. The nurse brought the perfect little boy for us to see, knowing that he could not live. Later we saw him again in his little white coffin before my father, the priest and the undertaker put him to bed in our cemetery, the youngest of all the dear dead, our small Saint Leo.

Mother's condition grew worse. Christmas was a heartbreaking day. Our washwoman came in and found me crying in the dining room. She asked the cause. "My mama is so sick," I answered, "I am afraid she is going to die." The priest and the doctor stood with father at mother's bedside. They looked at us three small children. "Doc," said the priest, "we can't let this little woman die." They didn't.

Tramps used to come quite commonly to our kitchen door in those days, asking for food. Ordinarily, mother or our hired girl would fix them a meal on the kitchen table. I was always incensed at their indigence and more than ready to send them on to earn their own living. This particular noon I saw one of these guests pass the dining room window. In a flash I jumped up saying, "Let me take care of him." My father, quicker, went to the door, brought the man in, seated him at the head of our table, and served him first.

One day in early June we were at table, just beginning dinner. Suddenly a luscious bird song broke the noonday quiet. Instantly, spontaneously the entire family were on their feet and out on the porch. In the near-by poplar tree, the first oriole of summer was telling us that he had returned.

The old ways and old days are over, irrevocable even to imitate, but dear to remember.

IV

United Nations

IN THE 1890's our empire builders began spanning our country west of the Mississippi with steel highways. Our great railway systems moved westward to the Pacific. James J. Hill brought a colony of laborers from southern Italy and Sicily to make the roadbeds and lay the tracks for the Great Northern Railroad. The wives and children of these men he settled in comfortable homes with good garden plots just south of Cumberland. Their family names read like an art catalogue: St. Angelos, de Riccis, Donatellos. A simple frame Church, St. Anthony's, constituted their spiritual capitol.

Eight miles south a robust German settlement flourished; east ten miles or more a smaller French colony. The pastor of our Saint Mary's Church in Cumberland had the spiritual care of these with the towns of Shell Lake and Spooner to the north in addition. This meant that we had Mass on Sundays on alternate weeks, sometimes only once a month. Families from south and east drove in to church through almost impossible roads and weather. Coffee and toast were always hot on our range for them before they started back home.

A significant fact is that the pastor of these United Nations had to be a linguist. During my childhood most of our priests were from Europe or had been educated there. Although we did not realize this, the culture of these pastors was not entirely wasted on us. Always at Sunday Masses we assisted at the Holy Sacrifice in Latin, and listened to announcements, Epistle and Gospel in English, French, German, Italian. This is quite a commentary on our heritage from the alleged low mentality of our Catholic immigrant ancestors.

No Catholic college for women existed in the United States before 1890. Very few parish grade or high schools existed in Wisconsin, none near enough for us to attend. Our religious instruction and our preparation for Holy Communion depended entirely on our pastor. Fortunately, a brilliant young priest, Father Stephen Leinfelder, educated in Rome, had been sent to pioneer in our north woods. His instructions for first Holy Communion were among the great spiritual and intellectual experiences of my life.

With no room in his house big enough for us to meet in, he took us into the church, seated us on the kneelers, transforming the seats into desks. Here we wrote down, at his careful dictation, the theology of the Blessed Sacrament. After an hour's work, always after school, we went home, copied our dictation carefully in ink and special notebooks and memorized the entire text. This was recited at class before the next dictation. Few children, I think, have ever been so honored in the quality of their instruction.

On the eve and the day of my first Holy Communion I surprised my parents with the only signs of asceticism they ever saw in me. Like most good German families we always ended our day with our glass of beer. This evening I walked quietly over to my father and mother to kiss them good night. "But you haven't had your nightcap," said my father in surprise. "I don't think I care for any," I said lamely. Mother helped me out. "Let her alone," she said, "if she wants to do this."

I had quantities of chestnut-colored wavy hair which I ordinarily wore down my back in curls. For fear I might be tempted to vanity on this greatest day of my life, I had my mother braid it tightly while all my little girl friends were transfigured in rag curls under their veils.

On May 29, 1898, our class received the sacrament of Confirmation. I had now reached the age of spiritual maturity.

V

Foothills of Parnassus

I WAS always the youngest and the smallest girl in my class. In the grades this meant a front seat and the automatic privilege of leading ranks as we marched around the room for exercise. In the big seats in high school it meant that my feet never touched the floor in the hours of sitting during my freshman year. The boys found this amusing until we began to work on algebra and Latin together. After that, they stopped teasing the littlest girl in high school.

Our high school offered two programs, one preparatory for college, the other terminal. As preparation for college we studied four years of Latin, two of German, algebra, plane and solid geometry, English, physical geography, botany, physics, history, constitutional government. Latin and German were my big intellectual experiences. Mathematics came next. The other subjects, I think because of the teachers, never came alive. My mother always described her children as "book and pencil crazy." I loved to read and always had my nose in a book. For all that, very little in my English classes stirred me except with indignation at the sarcasm of our teachers. It was a petty weapon to use against the unimportance of mere youth.

Our principals were always good, interested in all of us, identified with our work and our play. They gave us excellent talks at the opening sessions of the day. They contrived fifteen-minute free periods to read aloud to us: *Alice of Old Vincennes, David Harum, Main Travelled Roads*. They organized debating teams and brought the Lincoln-Douglas and Webster-Hayne debates to eloquent life.

Our schoolhouse was just a block from home on Back Street. It formed the center of our growing minds and activities in our early teens.

Saint Mary's Church was half a mile north on Front or Main Street. Some of our family went to Mass daily if our priest was not on a mission. During Lent we children all went every day. This meant early rising, breakfast, a race to our unheated frame church, often with the thermometer telling a true story of fifteen or twenty degrees below zero. We managed to make the Way of the Cross, assist at Mass, cover the half mile back to school before 8:50 A.M. What a marathon and with what enthusiasm and earnestness we made it!

Before my senior year a fine new school building was erected just across the street from our church. This simplified our difficulties in assisting at daily Mass. It expanded tremendously the facilities for good academic training. Declamatory contests were organized. Successful contestants went to county, and if surviving, to regional contests. I believe that I qualified for at least one of each.

Our schoolmates, with intense loyalty, went with us on these trips. We exhibited the same school spirit in accompanying our football teams to games with neighboring high schools.

The gymnasium of the new high school provided a fine basketball floor. Here, in copious woolen blouses and bloomers, we played boys' rules, at the peril of our lives.

Early in June, 1904, our class was graduated. Our commencement week included a class play in which I had a part against the leading man who was at the time immersed in romance with another girl. The impact of our performance was not over-whelming, I assure you. The conferring of diplomas climaxed the final evening on which we delivered our commencement essays. Our class numbered eight, I believe. We memorized our compositions and gave them without benefit of manuscripts or notable eloquence. Under the direction of my excellent German teacher I had written on "German Ballads and Folk Songs." This interested me particularly because my first attempt to write poetry was a translation of Goethe that I had quoted in this essay. I still find his lines very beautiful:

> *Über allen Gipfeln*
> *Ist Ruh'.*

The school year was over. I had been graduated from high school. Our parents had never promised us money. They had always promised us an education. I had some now. I was ready for more.

At the moment my father was building a new shop, still one of the substantial business buildings in Cumberland. Fred would be a sophomore at the University of Wisconsin. Mother used to tell us that our father pulled wax threads for all that we had. He needed time now to get ahead of inordinate expenses. So I stayed home for the year, kept the house, did the buying, meal planning for our family of four, and read Shakespeare some afternoons each week with our high school principal and two of my class-mates. Meanwhile, motorboats had come to our lake, dubious automobiles to our dirt roads. I did more than a fair share of riding in both. I was just seventeen and ready for the University of Wisconsin in September.

VI

Varsity, Varsity

WHEN, suddenly one day not too long ago, I asked myself, "Why didn't I go to a Catholic college for women?" I was faced with the fact that there were none, or practically none at that time, not at least within my geographical reach.

Adolescence had been filled for me with uncertainties, confusion. Why was I in existence at all? For what particular reason had God made me? What things were right or wrong? For whom and why? I was at odds with ambiguities. I wanted answers to be aye, aye and nay, nay. Applied to my intellectual life, I could not learn from my teachers exactly what was wrong with a composition, even a sentence. The immutable rectitude of the problem that I had solved correctly pleased me. The comment on my paper, "Try to improve this sentence," left me completely adrift. In the cause of certitudes, I elected mathematics as my major. Presently I found myself, with one or two other girls, in classes with engineers.

Professors Munro and Sellery gave that year what was for me a thoroughly satisfying experience in education. This in a lecture course on medieval history. But for me it meant art, architecture, evolving cultures, the Benedictine schools, the Crusades, the guilds. The great loves of my life are in so much of all this. Certainly, I have had more scintillating, more spectacular professors,

but none have ever taught me more. For instance, I, a freshman
from a microscopic town in the northern woods, was assigned for
a term paper, "A Commentary on the Rule of Saint Benedict."
At last I had come to a teacher who addressed himself to my
mind.

English, German, French, and the inevitable physical education completed my program. For one year I wrote three themes a
week, two prepared and one impromptu. All were corrected; all
were returned to us. A few were read aloud in class for criticism.
When the comments became too caustic, we girls who sat in the
front rows would all stare steadfastly at our instructor's feet.
This would set him pacing up and down the platform and relieve
our indignation. It was our only redress.

By the end of the year I knew the difference between a sentence and a paragraph, a comma and a semicolon, exposition and
narration. I had had English!

My brother lived with a group of boys, mostly Catholic, at 619
Francis Street. They, with some of my girl friends and me, used to
go together to Mass at Saint Patrick's on Sunday. A group of
South American, Mexican, and Filipino boys often joined us.
During the week Father Hengel, the chaplain for the Catholic
students at the University, gave us excellent instructions in
Catholic dogma. Mr. and Mrs. McCabe, a generous Catholic
couple, opened their beautiful home to us for dances once a
month. We had a fine sense of spiritual unity.

Within the year, the boys negotiated the purchase of the
former Chi Omega House on State Street for a Catholic student
center. The Chapel of Saint Paul came next in the organized
Catholic student life in Wisconsin. We were the pioneer group
in what are now the Newman Clubs on all our great university
and college campuses. My brother Fred and I take justifiable
pride in having helped to break the ground.

In his sophomore year, Frank Shroeder, one of Fred's engineer
classmates, had married a lovely girl from Philadelphia, a Quaker

at least one generation removed from the "thee" and "thou" Friends. They had an apartment on University Avenue. This became our social home. Only septuagenarians will remember the campus of my time when Chadbourne was the only residence hall for women with Miss Mayhew for its dean.

The Shroeders had their piano and music, their friends with violins. Mother used to send occasional boxes of "chicken and all that." University life could not have been more gracious.

Fred was a junior, which meant that I went with him to the Junior Prom. Clare Shroeder cared for me as her younger sister. We worked and played together. Fred and I used to take long walks on drizzly afternoons, browse in secondhand bookstores or tramp out to the University farm. Here a brilliant deaf and dumb research student used to take us around and in climax let us taste the cheeses.

We took the hurdles of fine concerts, lectures in French and German. Sarah Bernhardt came to Madison, playing in *Camille*. Thinking that Dumas was on the Index, I made the great refusal, not attending the performance. We did see "divine Sarah," made up like a French doll, driving through the Latin quarters and bowing graciously to students right and left. Imagine my amused astonishment at discovering the identity of *La Traviata*, which we invited to our campus in 1958, with the play that I had so conscientiously foregone as a coed.

The hours of most sustained interest were those spent at the University library. Here I had books, the reasons and the leisure to use them. One cannot overestimate what these mean to students at the precise moment that they are ready to learn.

The great teachers whom we knew or worked with still keep their achieved places: President Van Hise, "Sunny" Pyre, Karl Young among them. Professor Schlichter taught my brothers. His son, Sumner, our great economist of Harvard, was a curly-headed boy of seven or eight when we used to meet him playing on Lake Street.

VII

It Pays to Advertise

THE first summer home from college meant settling back into my place in my crowd, in town. We talked, danced, swam, motored by land and water. We rented a houseboat and for two weeks floated up and down the lake, fishing, swimming, just being, in the sun and under the long twilight evening skies. We came home bronzed with tan and starved for sleep.

The University had not become a conviction with me. One day I picked up the current *McClure's Magazine* in our nearest drug store. It carried the summer section on private schools and colleges. Set in the center of a page was this two-inch announcement:

> Saint Mary's College
> Notre Dame, Indiana
> A Liberal Arts College for Women
> For information address the secretary

Something extraordinary had happened. I bought the magazine, hurried home, sat on the back porch reading and rereading the simple statement. I said to myself, "If this makes a difference in my life I shall always remember it." Though there were only four of us at home I hid the magazine, terrified at the possibility of losing it. Some days later my mother said, "If you are going back to the University you had better be attending to your clothes." We had grown up making, pretty generally, our own choices and decisions. "I don't think I am going back to the University," I answered. "Where are you going?" came mother's astonished question. "To Saint Mary's College." Just like that! Mother was combing her hair and had it ready to twist into a French knot at the top of her head. Amazed, she loosed her hand and her pretty hair fell like a veil over her shoulders. "What do you think your father will say?" came next. "Oh! he will let me go," I assured her. He did.

I wrote a ridiculous letter to the Secretary, saying that I had completed a year at the University of Wisconsin, that I was accustomed to having my own way and a fair amount of social life; notwithstanding I wished to come to Saint Mary's in September. My absurd epistle remained unanswered. Instead, my parents received a most gracious letter in miraculous handwriting assuring them of my welcome and care for my well-being there.

The rest of this summer was busy with uniforms, table service, all the standard French boarding school appurtenances of 1906. Mother was in a daze of incredulous delight at her reckless daughter's electing a convent school. Father proudly displayed the beautiful letters from Saint Mary's to his most intelligent customers. He never lost that overwhelming pride in the college and the sisters.

Customarily, a graduate or a friend of the sisters met any students coming into Chicago. Darling Effie Ehrhardt met me, relayed me to a Cumberland boy who also met me, took me to lunch and put me on the train for South Bend.

Here a horse-drawn cab drove me out to school. Coming up the avenue I saw a sister of the Holy Cross for the first time. I observed mostly her cap and thought "How like a sunbonnet!" I was not enamored then nor am I now with the habit. Indeed, I have never seen a religious habit in which I would choose to spend the rest of my life for beauty's sake, spelling beauty with a small b. Arriving at Holy Cross Hall I felt that at least I was near to where I belonged. I had never thought that at Madison.

Although I had a transcript of A's and B's from the University, and despite my protest, I was put back into freshman English with sophomore English as a possibility. By Thanksgiving I was graduated from the freshman class. My dedication to mathematics was diverted. I signed up for Latin V, French II, German IV, Logic, Music; Christian Doctrine was a matter of course. My first hour in Latin V sounded serious and honest-to-goodness. At the end of the hour I went to Sister Angela, a Radcliffe graduate, and said, "This sounds hard." She said, "It is." "I think I will change to water colors," was my trivial commentary. I did. I have never ceased to regret that she or any of my teachers had not tried to find the possible student under the impossible girl and put me through a stiff course in the classics.

After the first semester in French at Wisconsin one translated rapidly and well either with preparation or at sight, or one did not recite at all. In consequence I was a prodigy to dear Sister Eugenie who did violence to her beautiful French by letting me teach elementary classes at times.

As I was growing up I found myself expecting to meet sometime a wonderful woman who would have a profound influence on my life. Knowing and loving Clare Shroeder I used to wonder if she might be the person. "No," I thought, "she was not enough older than I nor even enough wiser. I advised her as often as she counseled me." Now at Saint Mary's I went to my first sophomore English class. A sister about my own height came into the room, dark-eyed, straight-featured, quiet-mannered Sister Rita. She had just returned from Europe with Sister Irma and Elizabeth Jordan, the editor of *Harper's Bazaar*. Here was the long-awaited lady of my dream. Sister Rita had studied at Harvard, had had for friends, teachers, or both, Bliss Perry, Hamilton Wright Mabie, Charles Wells Moulton, Maurice Francis Egan, Charles Warren

Stoddard. Sister Rita, with the first Father John Cavanaugh, president of the University of Notre Dame, and Father Daniel Hudson, editor de luxe of the *Ave Maria,* formed the most brilliant triumvirate of teachers, writers, scholars that the two schools had known. Sister shared with us the riches of all these associations.

She always made our assignments for at least a month in advance. The wisdom of this period of gestation pleased me. As a teacher, I have always tried to imitate it. Lyric verse came as one of our first written exercises. With the immediacy of the confirmed extrovert I rushed up to Sister after class to tell her that I could not write poetry. She assured me that she knew that. Then I announced that I did not know what to write about. She suggested that I give some thought to the subject. My "German Ballads and Folk Songs" rushed into the vacuum. I had Goethe by the scruff of the neck. I would translate him. And though Sister laughed at my platitudinous version of his delicate German, I had come upon a manner of writing that I had never tried or been taught to use before. The discovery exhilarated me. After that I would lie awake at nights trying to fashion every lovely thing I knew into verse. I had found my medium.

Our English classes were conducted like seminars, around tables. Occasionally, after half an hour's lecture Sister would scatter current magazines on the tables and walk out of the room, leaving us to our own resources. Sometimes candy would substitute for periodicals. On her return she never found us in disorder. This is, I submit, one way of teaching English. I capitulated. Not that I loved mathematics less but that I loved English more.

As a child and a growing girl I had enjoyed an unusual degree of reasonable independence in my home. At public school and university we students collaborated in rather than surrendered to discipline. The French boarding school régime around which life at Saint Mary's moved presented more than one enigma to me. Loving the school, and with complete good will for all it wished

of me, I found myself a confused and involuntary nonconformist.
In freshman English I had read Robert Louis Stevenson. I subscribed to his statement that books are a mighty bloodless substitute for life. I agreed that hours of full free truancy under the
open skies are much more illuminating than incarceration in a dull
classroom. Putting the theory into practice, I discovered that our
prefect did not see eye to eye with R.L.S. and me. A girl was
dispatched to interrupt my enjoyment of the great out-of-doors
and to tell me that I was to go to class. "Tell Sister Claudia that I
am not going to class today" was my clear-cut, decisive reply.
Even now, at Saint Mary's this might amount to academic revolt.

Later, in the prefect's office, Sister asked the old, old question:
"Why did you come here to school if you did not expect to keep
the rules?" "Sister," I answered quite honestly and simply, "some
of the rules, I think, are rather foolish."

One case can stand for many. I made the dearest friendships of
my life during these two years. "Dix and the bunch" were and
are the rarest of persons. My marks were always well above ninety
—all except observance of rules. So at the end of two years my
record, printed in the bound volumes of the annual catalogues,
tells this story. My name appears as a student enrolled in the
college. Beyond that, I did not even qualify for honorable mention. All my friends were in the places of the elect. As a Saint
Mary's girl I was and am in Limbo.

Father Bertrand Conway, O.P., author of the *Question Box*,
gave the first retreat I had ever made. This was in late October,
1906. To me it opened spiritual worlds of which I think I must
have had some intuition, for which I know I had an immense and
clamorous hunger. For the first time the religious life was presented to my judgment and mind as well as to my emotions.
These told me that here was something that mattered, something
worth doing and being. "Why had God made me?" There were
all the classes I had cut, parties in my room, talking out of time
to bear testimony against me. Worst of all, I had never asked to be

admitted to the Sodality of Our Lady because I knew it would mean almost immediate expulsion. Pride recoiled from that. Clearly, the religious life was what I most desired and for which I had most completely disqualified myself. God did not make sisters out of girls like me.

VIII

Year of Decision

STOPPING to see friends in Madison on my way home in June I found that private boarding school had raised my social status. Grooming, posture, hairdress, manner were all not only commented on but commended. Saint Mary's was beginning to show. In Cumberland the same held true. For the first little while the girls were a bit stiff and aloof. Then they told me that they had expected boarding school to estrange me from them. In a moment we were all laughing at their mistake.

Father, mother, Vern and I were our whole family that summer. With considerable persistence I insisted that we speak German at our meals. We were a good conversational group and knew at least the difference between *essen* and *fressen*. No meals were spoiled, no great proficiency acquired; but at least our German did not atrophy.

At school our French classes had subscribed to weekly newspapers. Nothing in my education and his investment pleased my father more than my ability to read with ease my weekly French journal as he brought it to me from the post office.

Weeks passed; two at a cottage up the lake, two on the Mesabi Range where Fred was doing summer work in mining engineering. My wardrobe was put in order, luggage packed, and I was on my way to Saint Paul for a day's shopping en route to school. My train left shortly before midnight. Few porters were available at that late hour. Like the typical boarding school girl, I was loaded down with packages. A young boy offered to help me. On reaching my Pullman I thanked him and vainly proffered a tip. Taking off his hat, he said: "Gentlemen don't need no thanks." The gallant, albeit ungrammatical, idealism of that boy sent me happily back to college.

This year I returned as an old girl. Realities began to clarify, objectives to emerge. Sister Rita was still Sister Rita. I read seriously, discovered the first slender volumes of Alice Meynell and Francis Thompson. My neighbor across the hall used to light pink candles in the room and read Coventry Patmore aloud to me.

All summer I had gone to Holy Communion every Sunday and as often as possible during the week. This was not so normal then as now. By the very logic of eating three meals a day I began to go to Mass and Holy Communion daily. This meant rising at 5:30. Eileen Buddy Redmond, youngest sister of Bishop Charles Buddy, was my good friend in this. But always, always there was that unanswered question, "For what had God made me?" I had long since resolved that if I could only find out what, I would do it with all my might as long as I lived.

In desperation, I used to steal down to Sister Rita's classroom evenings to ask for help. At the door I would turn and go back to my room and my confusion. I knew that I would do whatever Sister told me to. Suppose I did what she wanted rather than what God wanted! No, I would take no chances even for her.

The Junior class had the questionable privilege of writing Memorial Day poems from which the best were selected to be read on the Memorial Day program. Mine was one of the two chosen that year. After the program I went up to the classroom of one of my teachers for a little visit. From her north windows I looked out at the novices and postulants at recreation. They were walking and talking together; a lively team was playing baseball. Again my old restlessness, "I wonder what I will be doing ten years from now," I said, half questioning Sister.

"I suppose if you thought that you might be a Sister you would be furious," was her astonishing reply. "Why, I would be the happiest girl in the world," I burst out with conviction, "but I know that I could never be a nun," with equal certainty.

One afternoon Sister and I walked on the river bank and talked of the religious life. No one had ever spoken of it to me before. I listened breathlessly, reverently. "I will do anything that God wants me to," I said, "if I can only find out what it is." "That is all that one needs for a religious vocation," was Sister's easy, simple answer. How it comforted me! She gave me an equally simple, easy booklet on vocation which was apocalyptic to me.

My brother was being graduated from the University of Wisconsin before our school closed. I was permitted to take examinations early in order to join my family at his commencement. When I went to tell Sister Rita goodbye she gave me an inscribed copy of *The Story of Fifty Years,* her own history of the Sisters of the Holy Cross. All the way on the train to Madison I read it like a starved person. Afterward, Mother told me that when I got off the train, despite my huge Merry Widow hat and smart clothes, she knew that I no longer belonged to them.

We dripped home by ones or twos from Madison, grandmother's and other tangential trips. I went up the lake to our cottage with our inseparable crowd of girls. I waited breathlessly for a letter from Sister Augustine. Finally it came. In substance, her instructions read that if I still thought as I did when last talking to her, I should write to Mother Barbara, the mistress of novices. This I did, telling her that I should like to enter the novitiate if and when she wished. These alternatives I volunteered: I might return to finish college. I might stay home for the year with my parents. I might finish school, stay home a year, and then enter. I might come at once. Or I might do none of these things. My absolute wish was to become a Sister of the Holy Cross. The decision she would make for me.

She wrote me to come at once, on September fourteenth specifically, and sent me a list of questions to answer. I mailed my reply on the feast of Saint Augustine, August thirtieth. I had two weeks in which to get ready.

IX

September 14, 1908

Such a wardrobe for a girl who had lived for clothes! And such subterfuges in buying black cashmere shawls and petticoats! Finally, the humorous little trousseau was in order. Not so my family! My father, not a Catholic, was sick with dismay. What had he done to me that I should want to leave him! Mother had too much of the fear of the Lord in her conscience to permit even a question. Fred felt himself treated as a rank outsider. This was the first major decision in my life that he had not shared. Vern was young and quiet and, I think, the nearest to being pleased.

My friends knew nothing of my plans. I thought that I would go, ostensibly back to school. I was almost sure that although I had been accepted in the novitiate I would probably be sent home. It might be better for my pride if dismissal came from the college rather than from the convent. I had refused ultrasocial invitations to house parties and the like; solicitous boy friends were more than curious as to my reasons. I would give them only half-answers. Late in the summer I put on my prettiest dress which Sister Cyril had made for the senior ball at Wisconsin. All blue voile and taffeta I went to my last dance with Vern. Only he and I knew that it was a valedictory.

September thirteenth was a bleak day. We were a bleak family.

Neither my deep nor my superficial joy could buoy them up. Traintime came and I was off. I cried in the Pullman most of the night at my father's helpless grief and Fred's blunt reproaches. Arrived at the Northwestern station in Chicago I ran over to the desk and wrote hurriedly:

Dear Papa,
       If you want me to I will come home.
                                   Sis

Before the letter could have reached him I was the gayest of postulants, having really come home.

Chicago almost undid me. The Saint Mary's girls were getting back to school. In my own great preoccupation I had forgotten that this was opening day. Half of my crowd were at the LaSalle Street station. We went down to South Bend together on the New York Central. But the questions! How much food was I bringing back? From whom had I heard? How had I spent the summer? Evasion characterized my answers to these and like queries.

In South Bend I had to buy two pairs of high black-laced shoes —I whose heart was in my regiment of assorted pumps and low shoes! How could I explain my new footwear to the crowd! Somehow I got a taxi to myself and drove to the shoe store and from there to the novitiate. Mother Barbara received me graciously. God had begun to answer my question. This was the fourteenth of September, the feast of the Holy Cross. I was going to be a Sister of the Holy Cross.

Canon Law was not as explicit then as now. I received the Holy Habit on December tenth and became Sister Mary Madeleva. My father humorously suggested "Model-Eva." The honor of bearing a combination of the names of the Mother of God, Magdalen, the friend of Christ, and Eve, the mother of mankind has always impressed me deeply. Father and mother came for the reception, fully expecting to take me home. Completely charmed and converted by their welcome, they spontaneously took Saint Mary's and our entire community to their hearts for life. I can think of no one who has loved us more.

I had been wearing my Holy Habit less than a month when Mother Barbara called me and asked if I thought I could teach a second academic class in English. Anticipating my life as a religious in the convent I had wondered what in the world the community could ever do with me. I was sure that I could scarcely wash dishes or sweep a floor well enough to be allowed to do either in the convent. I had never thought of being a teacher of any kind. But my answer to Mother was, "I will do my best." "You always do your best," she encouraged abruptly. I chronicle this as my one and only word of praise from her. Novices will appreciate its value.

The next morning, in a room before students, with books that I had never seen, I began teaching English.

The two years in the novitiate were devoted to the religious life: prayer, meditation, Mass, vocal prayers, the study and explanation of our Rules and Constitutions, all traditional and fairly standard in all communities. Meditation is an intellectual and spiritual activity that I have always loved. Whatever my imperfections in it, and they are many, it has never put me to sleep.

Studying our Rule took me straight back to the Rule of Saint Benedict on which I had written a term paper. Something more apocalyptic awaited me. At home we had an old German Lutheran Bible which my grandmother had brought from Europe. My father treasured it. Except for this I had never had a Bible in my hands. Mother Barbara took a small group of us for Scripture study. Fred sent me a Challoner-Douay Bible, which I still have, for Christmas. For two years we knew the joy of living with and loving God's words to us in that priceless class. I have much for which to thank my mistress of novices. For her Scripture class I think I owe the greatest debt.

Father had had garden tools and flower seeds sent out to us

from South Bend. With these we gardened during noon recreations. I used to say that I planted all my uncharitable conversations in our little plots. Spading, raking, hoeing have their values both for sanctity and sanity. Weeds are a fruitful subject for meditation.

Because of my brief period as a postulant I remained in the novitiate eight months after the end of my canonical first year. At the end of August, 1910, I exchanged my white veil for a black one and was sent to the convent to teach in the college and academy.

X

Teachers and Teaching

SISTER RITA died of cancer just after midnight on the morning of July twenty-third. It comforted me that she had stayed on to the end of the feast of Saint Mary Magdalen. She had sent word that she had almost gone to God that day to pray for me. She was just fifty. We had planned hours and walks together when my novitiate would be over. I am still waiting. I never knew her in the intimacies of community life. She remains still my dream-lady after all my seventy years. If she had them, I never saw her feet of clay.

Within that year, Sister Eleanore, the head of the philosophy department, and Sister Virginia, head of our voice department, died. They were three great teachers, three unforgettable women. All went to God with characteristic expedition, even shocking suddenness. They left no one even to approximate their statures. I was in the process of completing my senior class work. Classes in college English were being assigned me. Then classes in philosophy. By 1914 I was teaching juniors and seniors in English and philosophy. I was twenty-seven years old. By 1919 my repertoire included Scripture and contemporary fiction. Then I was sent on mission. Before changing the subject I want to say in praise of myself that at that mature age I introduced Dante and Newman's *The Idea of a University* into our curriculum.

Mother Pauline educated greatly in the magnitude of her aspirations for Saint Mary's and the quality of the teachers she invited to help her realize her dreams. In her hour of faculty bereavement great friends met the needs of the college. For a fortnight every year Dr. James J. Walsh lectured daily to the entire student body. We who sat at his feet still turn to him for information on everything that happened in the thirteenth century, America's first hospitals, and Dante.

For a like period Frederick Paulding, actor and critic, gave us at least one play or one contemporary novel a day. The actor presented the drama; the critic appraised it. So through the years we came to know the best of English, French, Italian, Russian and Spanish drama and fiction. If you were ever in his audience you remember the gloved elegance with which he presented the first fifteen minutes of his program. The removal of his gloves, he used to tell us, marked the beginning of real work.

William Baxter Perry, the blind pianist, cousin of Bliss Perry, performed and interpreted music in terms of colors, textures, contours that he had never seen. His sightless vision brought sight to our minds and ears.

During one summer Charles Seymour was guest lecturer in history. In those days he was professor at the University of Wisconsin. I can still quote sections of his lectures on Charlemagne and the Palace School. Because I was young and fairly responsible I had the privilege of bringing Professor Seymour to and from his lectures and providing him a collation of buttermilk. In 1935, when taking one of our sisters to Yale for graduate work, we reminisced in his office on his buttermilk days at Saint Mary's.

In 1911 a new religious community came into the life of the Church, dedicated at that time to the apostolate of the Orient. Father, later Bishop James Walsh came to Saint Mary's to

interest our students in his great mission. Again, as his official
escort, I shared his friendship until his death. Remembering his
graciousness, his greatness and humility, I am happy at our grateful return in the splendid Saint Mary's girls who now wear
the Maryknoll habit.

Under Father William Bolger, the University of Notre Dame
had developed an outstanding debating team. Father McGuire,
a brilliant Oxford graduate, teaching at St. Viator's College at
Bourbonnais, Illinois, had a team of matching brilliance. They
used to meet at the University for finals, putting on their pre-
liminary battle of brains and wit for the Saint Mary's students.
We young sisters were usually asked to act as judges. Here
through at least three college years we listened to young Fulton
Sheen. Even then we prophesied a brilliant future. We could
not have guessed its magnitude or its holiness.

Katherine E. Conway grew up in Rochester, New York. As
a girl she used to kneel beside young George Santayana in
church. She had the rare experience and training of working
with and for Bishop McQuade. She knew the rigor of his mind.
She learned from him the ideals of the educated Catholic, the
pattern of a great American clergy. Few girls in their early
twenties have been so fortunate. Once she submitted to the
Bishop a bit of writing into which she had grafted a bit of
French. He handed the manuscript back to her with the crisp
comment, "My dear, you will never have an idea that you
cannot express in English."

Among her reasons for going to Boston, two predominated.
She wanted to write and she wanted to work for the intellectual
life of the Church. Very soon her purposes and her personality
asserted themselves. Book-review groups, study clubs grew up.
Her own essays and poems got between boards. She lived for
a time in the home of Louise Imogene Guiney. Here was a
friendship of consequence. One day Louise brought home a
check for one hundred dollars for an article that had just come

out in the *Atlantic Monthly.* "That's a nice fat check, Louise," commented the literally poor Katherine. "Yes," replied Louise, "I read two hundred books to prepare the article and waited two years to have it published."

Eventually and for years Katherine was editor of the *Boston Pilot.* When John F. Fitzgerald became Mayor of Boston he invited her to manage and edit his paper. She accepted and continued in this capacity during all the years that "Honey Fitz" had need of this editorial service. Some of these were spent at Saint Mary's.

Miss Conway came into residence on our campus in 1912 as lecturer in Church history, Scripture, contemporary literature. She brought her lares and penates with her. These hung in photograph in her office, her household gods: Clarence Warren Stedman, John Boyle O'Reilly, James Jeffry Roache, Rose Hawthorne Lathrop among them. She was built into this group and remained one of them until her death.

Again, a cupbearer of the gods in a minor sense, I accompanied Miss Conway to and from class, took care of such messages and errands as she had need of. Walking with her, talking with her daily, reading proof, commenting on editorials, listening to her analysis of the Balkan and the First World War crises, I served a rich apprenticeship, such as few young teachers have known.

Rose Fitzgerald and Joseph Kennedy were married while she was at Saint Mary's. With a delicious appetite for romance, she savored vicariously the beatitudes of these nuptials. They could hardly have had richer fulfillment.

When Miss Conway left Saint Mary's in 1916, not to return, I found myself heir to her classes in Scripture and literature. The mantles of both Sister Rita and Miss Conway had fallen on my shoulders. I was not yet thirty. Young sisters are not necessarily either helpless or hopeless.

On a bright October afternoon Father John Cavanaugh (the

elder) came to the college with a young English convert and a
bodyguard of lesser celebrities. The guest of honor was Monsignor Robert Hugh Benson. For an hour he talked to us on
the elements of truth that give content and credibility to non-
Catholic and non-Christian beliefs. The lecture over, we left the
hall, silent, caught in the intensities of personality and conviction
that reassert themselves even in our memories of that hour. We
could not "come to" even with our closest friends.

Here again I was sent to take Monsignor Benson around such
parts of the college as might interest him. He followed my
youthful guidance with polite absent-mindedness. The less
either of us had to say at that moment surely was the better.
Only, as a woman, I remember his shiny cassock, his loose slip-
pers, the black cotton socks with narrow white stripes running
zebra-wise around his ankles. What curious nonessentials stick
in our memories!

He was to have returned for a series of Lenten lectures in
New York and then to have come on to us for a retreat. He died
of pneumonia in England in early December.

The impact of his mind, his conviction remain in the body
of his historical novels and his novels of the future. Our present
world crises and their ominous possibilities are all written down
in his *Lord of the World* and *The Dawn of All*.

If Saint Mary's could recall today those first fifteen years of the
present century it would find Christian Culture at the very core
of its curriculum.

XI

Great Things and Small

ONLY in long retrospect does one know and begin to understand the import of daily incidentals and unnoted odds through which the big ends of one's life are reached.

I had made my first profession, or temporary vows as we said then, on December 10, 1910. Fred had sent me a dozen lilies for my first Easter in the novitiate. White roses came for my first vows. One can say things with flowers!

Now one absolute theme dominated life. I would, if permitted, make my religious profession in the summer of 1914. It was a time of utmost earnestness, of ultimate giving and receiving for me. Our preparation was careful. Fifteen of us were to make our final profession before Holy Mass on August fifteenth.

The day was beautiful. Father and mother had come, now happy with and for me. When a young person, in a short, succinct formula, gives to God by vows pronounced in public, her whole life with all its promise, all its possibilities, little room is left for commentary. I had done this. I had given away everything that I had, or ever could have or be. I had come to the final answer. I had found out why God had made me. For Him and His reasons I had begun to be.

In 1915 I was permitted to make my first visit home with Sister

Fredrica, my German teacher, for companion. We stopped in
Watertown to greet my Lutheran grandmother. She found great
joy in having a dear little Berliner to speak German to her. In
Cumberland, the devout Italians kissed our hands, the Chippewa
Indians brought us wild berries.

In this and all subsequent visits we picked up friendships
where we had left off at our last partings. Few loyalties can
match the bonds and allegiances of one's home town. Cumberland has never failed me.

The summer of 1916 I spent with the Sisters of Saint Joseph at
their summer home on Lake George. One of our sisters and I
were their guests. Eddie Maginn, now the Most Reverend Edward Maginn of Albany, ran the motorboat for us. Perhaps he
remembers matching sonnets with me.

Father Thomas Verner Moore, just returned from Europe, was
living at the Paulist House, a quarter mile away. He and Eddie
piloted us on great hikes up Prospect Mountain. Although we
never did quite reach the top of the mountain, Father discovered
other heights of wonder and beauty to us which more than
compensated. You may recognize our guest as the eminent psychologist, now Fra. Pablo, a pioneer Carthusian in Whitingham,
Vermont.

Biennially, at least, I was permitted to visit my parents.
This afforded en route the hospitality of the Sisters of Saint
Francis in La Crosse, Wisconsin, and Winona and Rochester,
Minnesota; the Visitation Nuns in Saint Paul; the Sisters of Saint
Joseph at Saint Catherine's College; the good Benedictines at
Saint Scholastica's in Duluth. These colleges I have watched
grow to rich maturity with an almost maternal pride.

Usually, we either went home or returned by way of the
Great Lakes. "Nuns fret not at their convent's narrow room."

Multitudinous small odds one must read between all these
lines. The young sister is a magnet for jobs of many kinds. Be-
sides a heavy and mature teaching schedule I usually carried

additional and exacting loads of writing, sponsoring student publications, class organizations. Even with these, two bigger and
better extracurricular activities consumed the best of my own
personal intellectual life.

Four of us young sisters had been assigned to study for our
Master's degrees at the University of Notre Dame. These we
received in June, 1918. The experience, for all the pressures of
ways and means, amounted to mental luxury.

Young Father Charles O'Donnell, a Holy Cross priest of fine
scholarship and poetic gifts, was assigned to teach a summer course
in creative writing at Saint Mary's. His small class numbered
chiefly former Saint Mary's girls who had entered the community
and were not yet professed. By way of exploration, he assigned
us a sonnet to write. After class, he said to me, "If you can do
this you must have written other verse. Let me see some." The
next day he took my few simple lyrics and sent them to the
Atlantic Monthly.

Since that time I have been writing and publishing verse on a
slightly different basis. Two rules I set for myself at the very
beginning. I would publish under my religious name. I would
submit my work first to secular rather than to Catholic magazines.
I had heard so much about Catholics being unable to receive
recognition because they were Catholics. I resolved not to permit
mediocrity in my writing to be attributed to my religion. As a
Catholic and a sister I would write well enough for acceptance
by the secular press, or I would not write at all. The old *Bookman*,
now discontinued, published some of my first verse. *American
Mercury, Saturday Review of Literature*, and *The New York
Times* have accepted my small output.

For this same reason my manuscripts for books have been
submitted first to secular publishers. Appleton-Century and
Macmillan accepted these immediately. Having laid the ghost
of rampant discrimination against Catholic writers I got into my
own Church and my own pew. The *Catholic World, The Ave*

Maria and *Spirit* have been very kind to me. Saint Anthony Guild Press and Sheed & Ward have more than matched them.

I write these things for what possible help they may provide to young religious more gifted and less enterprising than myself. They can scarcely be more fortunate in friendships. More than once Joyce Kilmer came with Father O'Donnell to visit. They shared with me their clear, incisive poetic insights. Their minds were quick with poems waiting to be written. The importunities of war pressed. Both men volunteered for service. Both went overseas. Joyce was killed in action on July 30, 1918, near Ourcq in France and buried beside a stream that bears the same name. Father blessed his grave before coming home. Aline, his wife, and I corresponded occasionally until her death. The children, Sister Michael, the Benedictine daughter, and Kenton with his artist-wife and children I prize as friends.

Given these and other almost equally stimulating contacts, relationships, the hungry reading of poetry for beauty's sake, the constant, restive desire amounting to an imperative need to write, with no time, no leisure, no freedom from the pressure of persons and things, what was I to do?

My subconsciousness must have had a multitude of occupations. Intellectual and emotional impacts were intense. Living in boarding school provided no outlets. Insomnia came as a solution. A sonnet and a short lyric good enough for immediate publication were not infrequently the fruit of one sleepless night. Exhaustion was inevitable.

And then on the night of the feast of Saint Ann, 1918, I was taken by ambulance to Saint Joseph Hospital for an emergency appendectomy. Peritonitis and no sulfas left small margin for recovery. But after seven weeks I got into my shoes, learned to walk again, and returned to school.

In August, 1919, my good superiors sent me on mission to Sacred Heart Academy, Ogden, Utah. I was elated. Mountains at last! Deserts, sagebrush, the West! Oh, pioneers!

XII

The West and I

THE theory of religious life submits the proverb that the happiness
of a convent depends on the superior and the cooks. Sisters Celsus,
Anicetus, and Felicitas put halos around this proverb. With
them in these key positions, Sacred Heart Academy in Ogden became my happiest mission.

Among our hundred and twenty boarders, fewer than thirty
were Catholic. Most of them were Mormon children. In Ogden,
the Mormons placed major emphasis on the arts. They sent their
daughters to convent schools for these. Consequently, ballet and
interpretive dancing comprised our entire program in physical
education which concluded with an ambitious pageant at the
end of every school year. Practically everyone studied at least
one musical instrument. I have attended concerts by our students
at the old Salt Lake City Theater with seven harps on the stage
for ensemble numbers. Speech and drama flourished. Our high
school students regularly presented Yeats, Synge, Lady Gregory,
contemporary American plays. They gave a fine out-of-door pro-
duction of *A Midsummer Night's Dream*. I found more than
mountains and sagebrush in Ogden.

On my first errand downtown I stopped at Spargo's Drug and
Bookstore. Bernard De Voto, a junior at Harvard, was working

47

there for the summer. Mother Augusta, one of the Sisters of the Holy Cross who nursed soldiers of North and South during the Civil War, was at its close in 1865 in charge of a hospital in Cairo, Illinois. On leaving there she brought with her the two De Voto children, Flo and Rose, orphaned by the war. Flo she had sent through law school at the University of Notre Dame; Rose was graduated in music at Saint Mary's.

When Mother Augusta went to Utah in 1875 she urged these two brilliant young students to join her. Flo began law practice in Ogden where he remained all his life. Here he married and here Bernard was born. The first eight years of his school life he spent at Sacred Heart Academy. He had the questionable distinction of being the only little boy admitted to this select academy for young ladies. I cannot say that Bernard relished the privilege. When I met him he was in the process of achieving Harvard's intellectual maturity and writing the first of his novels.

The plans of more than one of his projected books we took apart and put together again across the bookstore counter at different times during my years in Ogden. Through all his turbulence of mind and soul we remained friends. He wrote me once, "I am one of that unhappy band whose minds refuse the allegiance without which their hearts will never be at rest." His last letter came a matter of weeks before his death.

Gladys Rich, a graduate of the academy and a gifted musician, was at this time the president of our alumnae association, with Jule Kiesel McGinley our most indescribable exponent. Jule outmeasured types and standards. She explains, in part at least, her daughter Phyllis. What rewards they were for each other!

Phyllis and Gladys, sorority sisters at the University of Utah, spent hours of their vacations at the Academy. Far after convent hours, we raced into Phyllis' smart verse, played and hummed through musical comedies done in collaboration for university song fests or future classroom programs. *The Good Ship School, The Pink Huzzar, Lullabies from Many Lands* were all in the making then, some at least to be published by Schirmer later. Phyllis' gay, heady gift troubled me. I was almost afraid to tell her how good it was. I hesitated to recommend the *Smart Set* as an avenue of publication. But she was Jule Kiesel's daughter. I need not have worried.

One pretty afternoon Mary Matson came to my classroom with her brother Mark and Jimmie Keller, his roommate, visiting him from Saint Mary's College, Oakland, now Morago County. Mary and I, as student and teacher, friend and friend, have shared many fine things. Jimmie Keller is one. We had a happy afternoon, falling easily into the pattern of college talk. Weeks later Mary rushed into my classroom again with a letter which she thrust into my hand with "Read it, Sister." I did. Its story runs briefly thus:

> Dear Mary,
>
> I have been thinking a good deal lately. We have only three score and ten years to spend in this business called life. I have decided to invest mine in the stocks that pay the highest dividends. I am going to Maryknoll.
>
> Sincerely,
>
> Jim

Already you may have recognized in this keen young appraiser of stocks and bonds the future Father James Keller, M.M. and founder of the Christophers.

You may wonder when between these delectable interludes I taught anybody anything. Be assured that even then I attempted, as I still say facetiously, to work twenty-five hours out of twenty-four. Recently a former Ogden student visited Saint Mary's. For all her earnest study while at school she found the intellectual life most difficult. Wisely, she wrote me in her bread-and-butter letter after her visit, "Sister, don't worry about the grades your students receive. Wait thirty or forty years and then ask them what you taught them. They will remember."

My first Ogden vacation I spent with my parents for what seemed a necessary rest. The second summer Mother Perpetua, Sister Rita's dearest friend, invited me for her sake to Saint Agnes Convent, Los Angeles. Here I taught a bit to justify my traveling expenses; I read *The Love Letters of Elizabeth and Robert Browning*. I wrote poems on "The Pepper Tree," and other verse still surviving in my *Collected Poems*. I spent the fourth of July at Carmel. St. Catherine of Siena had already told me something of the "Sea Pacific." Here I had the wonder of the Pacific Ocean at my feet.

In the spring of 1922 Sister Celsus, still my religious superior, told me that I was to go to the University of California, Berkeley, for a summer session of graduate work in English.

XIII

"Sudden the Worst Turns the Best"

BY CHOICE, I registered for a Chaucer course to be taught by John Livingston Lowes, rare teacher and rare friend from Harvard. By the worst of mistakes, I blundered into a seminar of Nineteenth Century Ideas, the only subject in the program that I knew I did not want. Professor Benjamin H. Lehman, brilliant young student-friend of Professor Lowes, was teaching the course.

Arriving at the right room on the wrong day, I found the place packed. I squeezed in. Professor Lehman arrived. "Obviously," he said, "we shall have to begin by eliminating. Auditors must go first. How many have bachelor's degrees?" I raised my hand. "Master's degrees?" Again, I raised my hand. By this time the survivors did not constitute a crowd. "How many are working for Doctor's degrees?" Without knowing whether I was or not, and with an impulsion quite outside my will, I raised my hand. I—medievalist by every attraction—had got myself into Nineteenth Century Ideas.

We were less than a dozen students at the final screening. Our whole summer's business consisted in selecting a proper subject and submitting it in a proper paper for discussion, revision, and possible survival. Discussion meant literary surgery, acute, caustic,

penetrating. My paper had been scheduled for the first session of
the fourth week of school. There might have prevailed some slight
curiosity as to the kind of paper a nun would turn in. For me, the
three weeks of waiting were an unmitigated reign of terror. I had
been away from college for three years, away from its manner of
thought and speech. My three weeks in the seminar had been
exacting. Every graduate student knows the story. I was among
strangers.

I had selected for my subject, "The Prose of Francis Thompson
as Transitional from Coventry Patmore to Gilbert K. Chesterton."
My confreres in Nineteenth Century Ideas knew not one of these
great captains of thought. The afternoon for my paper came.
For thirty minutes I read on without interruption. The bell rang.
I stopped. "Go on," said Professor Lehman. After a bit I interrupted myself to apologize for keeping the class overtime. "We
are willing to stay," I was assured.

When I had finished Professor Lehman said, "This paper is
practically ready for publication. I could not have done it," and
dismissed the class.

This was the year during which Professor Lowes was immersed in his great work, *The Road to Xanadu*. Like Mary's lamb,
wherever Chaucer went, Coleridge went, too. For my particular
job in research a study of Chaucer's Nuns from inside the convent seemed ideal and opportune. Here again my paper was pronounced ready for publication when Professor Lowes returned
it to me.

During the year the entire output of my first summer session at
Berkeley had earned its living through publication in various
issues of the *Catholic World*. My mission was changed from
Ogden to Woodland, California, just three hours' train ride
from Berkeley. Signs began to point to continued graduate work.
But not without a severe tertianship at Holy Rosary Academy
with Mother Barbara for my superior.

The Berkeley Summer Session Bulletin arrived in early March,

1923. Henry Seidel Canby was to conduct a program in critical writing for a group not to exceed twelve. Applicants would be chosen on the merits of published or unpublished work. No applications would be considered after April fifth.

During the past years I had got my accumulating verse together under the title *Knights Errant and Other Poems,* had sent it off to Appleton's who had accepted it. Mother Barbara had always encouraged me to write. The Appleton approval pleased her. No one needed help less than she in deciding what any of her household was to do at any time. Consequently, I had not mentioned the attractive Berkeley program to her. She asked me. Mr. Canby's course she thought most geared to my possibilities. I pointed out that the application was already two weeks late. Nevertheless, she told me to apply.

What with two critical articles published within the year and a book of verse in galley proof, I was admitted to the course.

Our group of twelve made headlines in the campus publications the summer long. Papini's *Life of Christ,* Gertrude Atherton's *Black Oxen,* Eleanor Wylie's *Black Armour,* Edna St. Vincent Millay's *The Harp Weaver and Other Poems* all came out that summer. Some of the books we read before they got between boards.

Our job consisted in selecting three books each, reading and writing a critical review of each of them. With a list of a dozen books just coming off the press we would produce about three reviews of each from which to choose the best. Mr. Canby read them aloud. The class criticized and then chose what they considered might eventually appear in a hypothetical critical literary weekly. This was the *Saturday Review* aborning. Our seminar provided the incubator. The class chose all three of my criticisms for the unborn magazine.

When my article on Edna Millay, "Where Are You Going, My Pretty Maid," came out, Bernard De Voto wrote me pages of congratulation. The Catholic mind had found a nun for an exponent. The first critical article on Edna Millay had appeared. This pleased Bernard, sensitive and unnecessarily embarrassed over Catholic illiteracies of all sorts.

I had planned a comparative study of Emily Dickinson, Edna Millay and Eleanor Wylie and had completed the reading when time ran out. I have often regretted missing so golden an opportunity. The Dickinson revival had not yet begun.

For two years I commuted from Woodland to Berkeley in a breathless biweekly schedule. During my final year I lived in San Francisco and crossed the bay in the dear obsolete ferryboat every day. That in itself, with sea gulls, impenetrable fogs, the tang of the Pacific, irrepressible student passengers from the other side of the bay, provided surcease from the spasms of panic, the chronic "if I fail" state of mind which all but overwhelmed my waking hours. One hurdle after another was taken. Examinations were finally over, my dissertation approved. The Appleton-Century Company had already accepted it. Otherwise the University of California had volunteered to publish it. The fact that Benjamin Kurtz had written the foreword caused a bit of an academic breeze. I was informed that before my advent he had never admitted a sister to any of his classes. More than one letter to me he signed "Your professorial sinner." The three-hour public oral examination was in those days the last and worst of all the academic game. Until that feast of Saint George, 1925, no sister had qualified for a Doctor's degree at Berkeley. My orals must have occasioned some curiosity. When I came into the room with my committee even the hall outside was crowded.

In commending me afterward, one professor said, "The thing that came through to all of us most clearly was that you were sustained by something beyond mere academic competence." Looking back now, all seems to have moved in quiet, ordered inevitability. The business of living through day after unpredictable day as an intellectual and ascetic experience makes wearing pebbles in one's shoes a fairly comfortable alternative.

Saying goodbye, my professors asked what I planned to do now.

"Go home and save my soul," came the prompt reply. Then I enlarged: "You may have thought that being out of my convent on a big co-educational campus was quite a lark. Nothing in these past years has been so hard as separation from my community, my sisters, my proper life."

One dear old professor who had at times been quite a gadfly to me pulled my sleeve and confided, "I think I understand." This was April 23, the feast of Saint George. Other dragons might be lying in wait, but not today. California was a heaven of peach and almond blossoms. How could I have written a whole big book, a dissertation on *Pearl: A Study in Spiritual Dryness.* The Dark Night had passed.

For more than thirty years I have lived away from Berkeley and far from California. In 1949 my Alma Mater invited me to lecture at summer session. I was welcomed back with such gentilities of culture as only Ben Lehman and Guy Montgomery could command. Even more recently, old teachers and new have shared tea and the luxuries of reminiscences with me, Professor Lehman again being our perfect host.

Two years ago in Los Angeles the English faculty of the graduate school of the University of Southern California invited me to a charming luncheon and an afternoon on campus. All this came as a courtesy from a sister graduate school to a graduate of Berkeley.

Crossing the bay for the last time in the dear old ferryboat, I wrote a valedictory which I called "Patrins." In it I tried to say goodbye for many goods. These are the first lines of my attempt:

> "Yes, I shall leave these patrins as I go:
> Plucked grasses here, a few blown blossoms there,
> To tell you, though I've gone, how much I care;
> To tell you, also, should you want to know,
> The way I've taken, my beloved, so
> That you can find me, find me anywhere."

So, here I am, Berkeley.

XIV

On Incubating a College

On an early morning in September, 1926, you might have seen the recently qualified Doctor of Philosophy from Berkeley piled in among the first load of furniture going up to our new school on the east bench of the Wasatch Range, two miles from Salt Lake City. The old Saint Mary's Academy, once in the finest residential section of the city, was no longer safe or suitable for a boarding school for girls. The intermountain area needed a Catholic college for women, Bishop Glass argued. At his advice, this most majestic of sites was purchased and an imposing college built. Just a week before the opening of classes we began the transplanting.

Out of many comedies of many errors we gradually arrived at solutions. My problem was to create a college where no college had ever been. We began with the library. Before we had the windows and the books in the section assigned to the library we had invited to our faculty the best librarian we could find in the West. This precedent has become a law of the school. We assigned to our classes in religion the first and best hour of the day. We set up a program of school officers and such form of student government as the students themselves supported. We published our program of extracurricular activities well in advance each semester.

Every Sunday afternoon we served tea from two to five for all the household and any guests who happened to call. Frequently, we walked in groups up the mountainside and back, returning in the evening to make hot chocolate in the social hall before going to bed. More frequently, we read aloud from Ogden Nash, P. G. Wodehouse, *Green Pastures,* and such gay comedy. Many of our girls were musically gifted. There were few songs for which someone could not improvise piano and violin accompaniments. Capitalizing on the smallness of our college, we could have waffle breakfasts with no trouble at all. Often and often we hiked up the mountains, built our fires and cooked Denver sandwiches in the snow. The amenities of our lives would have been impossible almost anywhere else.

Our faculty was better than good. In a national science contest open to all college freshmen, our three contestants won a first, a second prize, and an honorable mention out of a total of eighteen awards. In the state board examinations for teachers' licenses, our students ranked highest in the state. In a student body of fifty, seven read the entire *Beowulf* in Old English with me and liked it. We wrote and produced our own musical comedies: *Twenty-one Eves and an Adam,* and *China Blue.* We presented the best trilogy of English mystery plays that I have ever seen. Our other dramatic productions matched these in quality and taste.

A large and rare collection of European art, assembled by Bishop Glass and housed at the college, made the school an art museum.

Lew Sarett and Louis Untermeyer visited and talked with us of poetry. Seumas MacManus spent more than one fortnight bringing us the authentic and all-but-lost epic art of the shanachie. When lecturing at the University of Utah, Professor Lehman shared his gifts of critical thought with us also. His appointment as Bishop of Great Falls brought that dearest of all friends, Bishop Edwin O'Hara, to the West. He came to the Wasatch frequently with problems of educational organizations, of nursing education, of Confraternity of Christian Doctrine study clubs. Every visit was an event. The University of Utah collaborated with us at all times, providing teachers, sharing guest-artists, inviting us to participate in its programs.

One of our students had entered as a junior from the University. This meant that we had our first college graduate in 1928. If there had been a class of one hundred instead of one the program could not have been planned with more dignity. Baccalaureate Mass in the beautiful Cathedral of the Madeleine, academic procession, the investing in the Bachelor's hood, and conferring of the degree all unfolded in medieval pageantry the life of the mind. Faye Eliza Williams was the first to receive a Bachelor's degree from the newly-founded college. Today, she is among its best-loved alumnae.

Very early in the spring of 1933, Mother Vincentia, our Superior General, wrote instructing me to be ready to leave for Europe the following summer. I was to spend a year observing and studying colleges for women abroad. Term times, if possible, should be kept for Oxford. In late May, I said my farewells to our infant college.

Seven of the best years of my life had been invested there. We had often been cold, sometimes hungry. Coyotes had cried under our windows at night. Water shortages had left us parched and unwashed during all but unbearable months in summer. Once at least every winter we were snowed in, cut off completely from Salt Lake City by wind-driven mountain snows. Days at a time we lived literally in the clouds and above the clouds. We watched weather in the making: rivers of sand flowed for days across Salt Lake Valley; canyon contours changed entirely as cloudbursts hurled mountainsides of shattered rock into them. We followed the silver path of the sun in its setting behind the mountains beyond Great Salt Lake. After its long rose-colored afterglow, two firmaments awoke in the darkness: the stars above us and the twinkling lights of Salt Lake City and its five suburbs covering the valley below.

Most magic of all was the mystery of full moonrise over our high eastern horizon, prefaced by a half hour of heralding light, then the moon a silver line, a quickly growing surface, a completed sphere. While watching this phenomenon of magnitude and splendor we caught something of our own dizzy daily journeyings around and around. I have watched moonrise on the Great Lakes, on sea and ocean. Full moon over the Wasatch mountains always answers in an enchanted affirmative my question, "Do I love mountains better than oceans?"

The western parks—Yellowstone, Bryce, Zion, Grand Canyon —were within easy driving distance from the college. We took groups of students to at least one of these each summer. What an exchange of campus, classrooms and books! Yellowstone the very fulfillment of Scriptural text: Wisdom, playing in the world: whose delights were to be with the children of men. Only God could make such a playground.

Just outside the west gate the unforgettable Tetons bit high horizons into the blue with their grim gray mountains. The Snake River ran clear and ice-cold at their feet.

Bryce was another of wisdom's playgrounds for children of men, wind-carved into a myriad majestic forms from buff and tawny and burnt orange sandstone.

We stood dwarfed and impotent before the majesty of Zion, its great white throne, its altar of sacrifice. No one tries to find words for Grand Canyon. Each time we returned to this tremendous wonder, we paid it the same perfect tribute of silence. Always in the parks, the desert, the mountains we found ourselves at school in the original and best sense of the word: at leisure to learn and to be taught. For seven years, Saint Mary-of-the-Wasatch was more than a school, more than a convent, more than a home to me. It was my self. It will always be difficult for me to think objectively of it.

XV

I Enter Oxford

Two facts were pretty clear in our minds. We were to spend a year in Europe, Sister Verda Clare at the Sorbonne perfecting her French, I at Oxford perfecting my English. We each had one thousand dollars. When that was gone we were to come home. In our devices to economize we laughingly proposed cutting our postage stamps in two.

From two apparent casualties resulted the two major joys of my year. We missed our first and best boat reservation. This committed us to the *Aurania*, sailing from Toronto on September 1. Madge Vaison, the secretary of Charles Du Bos, the prince of French intellectuals, was on board. Immediately she looked us up. Immediately we entered upon one of my happiest friendships. We talked, walked, prayed together until Sister and I landed at Plymouth. There Madge's clerical cousin directed us to a convent for lodgings. On the earlier boat that we had planned none of this would have happened. Now it is difficult to imagine my life without the dear love of Madge and her family, the profound affection of Charles Du Bos and all that his thinking, his teaching have meant to Saint Mary's, to Notre Dame and to me. Accidents are so often God's way of being doubly good to us.

After a night and a day in Plymouth we went by bus to Exeter for another day, then on to Buckfast where we sat in the chair of Abbot Vonier, to Torquay, to London. We arrived at 11 Cavendish Square about nine o'clock the evening of September 13, the vigil of the feast of the Holy Cross. By nine in the morning we were on a tuppenny bus for the Haymarket, Westminster Hall, Westminster Cathedral, returning to the convent after having seen in our first three hours more of London than some of the sisters had seen in years. Sunday we drove through Hyde Park, Kensington, Kew Gardens, to Richmond. While falling short in my appraisal of its historical realities I did understand its world of Michaelmas daisies. Every garden spot was banked with them.

We left by train for Canterbury. Here were Chaucer, Saint Thomas à Becket, Dickens, Joseph Conrad, the graves of Saint Augustine and Queen Bertha, Christian England measured in a span. We left by train to Dover, on to Calais, to Brussels. Liège, Louvain, and Aachen were meccas each in its own right. Cologne was restive and terrified. Troops of children drilled in the streets after school. One asked questions in whispers, fearing that even then, in 1933, the walls had ears. Loving German hospitality, the kind sisters, the dear children who took our hands and kissed our crucifixes, we were, nevertheless, glad to reach Paris where things were less ominous.

Here, presently, we were at 4 Rue des Deux Ponts on the Ile St.-Louis. We were at the home of Charles Du Bos. Here you must permit me the luxury of a digression for what has become the very warp of my life.

"Charles Du Bos, gentle and accomplished man of letters, with his charming wife, Zezette, lived on the Ile St.-Louis, in beautiful rooms overlooking the Seine and the Choir of Notre-Dame. There at carefully selected gatherings, small tea parties or smaller luncheons, I met many well-known

authors, poets, novelists, and literary celebrities of every
sort. For, somewhat like Nadia Boulanger, Du Bos has
devoted his life to his enthusiasm for the work of others.
François Mauriac, Paul Valéry, André Gide, Paul Bourget,
Hugo von Hofmannsthal, Rainer Maria Rilke, and a host of
others were all his good friends, and held his opinion in
high esteem. What good talk there was and how pleasant
to listen to, while the river flowed under the bridges gleam-
ing in the afternoon light as the spires and buttresses of
Notre-Dame grew darker against the western sky."

This paragraph from *Autumn in the Valley* by Mrs. Winthrop
Chanler epitomizes the manner and life and work of this rare
scholar who has come to be accepted as one of the finest critical
minds of our time.

Charles Du Bos was by vocation a lover of letters, a disciple of
words, as of the Word. In all surroundings, he gravitated naturally and always to the deep seriousness of the student. This over
the period of a lifetime resulted in the profound acquirements of
the scholar. The scope and penetration of his learning were its
obvious dimensions. Holiness was its essence. The story of all this
will some day be unique biography. Meanwhile something can
be done by way of appreciation.

One may well begin at the beautiful apartment at 4 Rue des
Deux Ponts on the Ile St.-Louis. This had been for many years
the home of the Du Boses and a rare literary center of Paris.
Here, by gracious appointment or happy invitation, came writers,
artists, pilgrims, from the cultures of all the world. Entering
the living room, they found themselves immediately in a home
of beauty, in a dwelling of the mind. They felt themselves uplifted and upheld by truth. Below and in the immediate fore-
ground, they saw the Cathedral of Notre-Dame, its apse and
delicate spire tranquil above the busyness of the river and the
world. This was something more than landscape. It was the vital

center of the Du Bos home. Every day began with the seven-
thirty Mass in the Lady Chapel of the Cathedral. Every Mass
terminated with the kiss of peace exchanged between the quar-
tette that composed the family, Charlie and Zezette, Primerose
and Madge.

Beyond the living room lay that world of books, the library.
Here one found Charles Du Bos truly at home. A deference
finer than the grace of the French gentleman characterized his
welcome to his guests. He seated them close beside him, then
met their minds with a dignity worthy of his own. The rows and
piles and shelves of books gave outward manifestation of that.

Charles Du Bos had been a student at Oxford in 1900, at
Florence in 1904, at Berlin in 1905. Apart from his exhaustive
knowledge of French thought, he was a profound student of
English, German, and Italian literature, and lectured brilliantly
in all these languages as in his own. The word "profound" must
be understood to indicate a depth amazing in its exhaustiveness
and penetrating in its clarity. It included a preparation simultaneously philosophical and literary. Bergson was the teacher
out of his own century of whom M. Du Bos spoke with deep
affection as one who had influenced him most. Saint Augustine
was his greater and even more beloved master.

Looking about his library, one got a bewildering sense of the
scope of his interests and of his studies. He read always the best
in current literature and one may say he read the best out of
current literature. He read back into the nineteenth and eighteenth centuries with scrupulous thoroughness and understanding. He gave himself with peculiar philosophical competence to
the study of Goethe. His intellectual devotion went to Walter
Pater and his love to Keats. He interpreted Pascal with deep
spiritual sympathy. His lectures on the Brownings and on
Claudel are unforgettable.

Out of this world of books grew the life of M. Du Bos, for he
gave more than a good half of his time and strength to intense

creative criticism of the writing of the last three centuries. This he dictated for the most part in French. A study on Walter Pater he had planned to make simultaneously in English and French. His long study of Byron has been translated into English. A series of lectures given in English at faculty meetings at Saint Mary's College under the title, "What Is Literature?" and published by Sheed & Ward he dedicated to us. His essays as a whole are published in Paris (usually by R. A. Correa) under the general title, "Approximations." There are seven volumes of these. They include studies of Patmore, Charles Morgan, Baudelaire, Tolstoi, Hardy, Maurice Baring, Thomas Mann, John Middleton Murry, André Maurois. His *Le Dialogue avec André Gide* and *Le Problème du Romancier Catholique* are separate volumes. Here, altogether, one has what may easily come to be accepted as some of the best critical writing of our century. But it is less by this than by his diary, that intimate chronicle of his prayers, his daily communion with God and man entitled *Extraits d'un Journal*, that his place is assured in the memory of men. This is as he had wished. There is also a body of unpublished work that will be of the first importance.

Through his *Journal* one sees pass the unique and reverent procession of his friends. They came to him from all worlds, from all ages, and in every need. His friend, François Mauriac, wrote of him:

> "No one during these last years met him without being helped. With what charity, what respect, he received the confidences of human love! What welcome waited those who brought their griefs to him, and how the wind of grace blew wide his door! He responded to every appeal, nor repulsed a single hand extended to him."

Naturally his world of literary associates was wide and rich. For thirty years Edith Wharton was his devoted friend. A picture of her taken at the age of ten stood on the desk in his daughter's room. One recognized in it the lovely oil painting which hung in Mrs. Wharton's study at Hyères. André Maurois, T. S. Eliot, Thornton Wilder, Desmond Fitzgerald, Frank Sheed, were, from various continents, of his world and mind. On his visits to America, the Abbé Dimnet visited the Du Boses whom he described as "Babes in the Woods." One of them, he said, "is a genius." Gertrud von Le Fort, the German novelist and poet, was for many years close to his life. An attempt at enumeration is useless. Mrs. Chanler's is a fair cross section of the intellectual group that shared the friendship of Charles Du Bos. In that group none were more intimate than the Maritains, Jacques and Raïssa.

In 1937 the Reverend John O'Hara invited M. Du Bos to come to the University of Notre Dame as a guest professor. He became even more a beloved teacher and friend to all faculty and students at Saint Mary's. Two incidents out of that experience, unacademic though they be, describe the man abundantly. When his train reached South Bend he had already been identified by the Pullman porter who had seen his picture in the morning paper and accorded him all the deference due the very great. His clear, kind blue eyes, his drooping moustache, his student's shoulders, his cane, all came almost immediately to characterize this gentle European scholar in a most American environment. Committed by the porter to the Midwestern scene, he went with his family at once to his temporary home on Peashway that grew dear to him with intense and intimate associations. He lunched at Saint Mary's and then arranged immediately for daily Mass and his weekly confession. Only after these had been provided for beyond mishap did he advert to his academic program and schedule. In 1927 he had had the overwhelming experience of religious conversion. His spiritual director, the Abbé Altermann, had advised the practice of daily Mass and Holy Communion, and he obeyed with tenderness and tears.

During these years, Saint Mary's was more than home to

"Charlie" and his family. Every morning we met at Mass at which he assisted, often in tears. Breakfast followed. Then came our conversations in my office—Charlie on one side of the table with his innumerable pipes, I on the other. One pipe after another was lighted, smoked and cooled as we talked of ominous world conditions, the epistle or gospel of the Mass of the day, a current book, a line from Julian of Norwich, the light that is life. You can easily guess that my contributions to these conversations were chiefly monosyllabic. Charlie needed oral expression and a listener before he fixed his clarities of thought into the clarities of prose. His inscriptions in all his books on my special Du Bos shelves tell something of this exchange. Not even the experience, as the lived life of which he loved to speak, submits itself to adequate exposition. I can only say I am a different I because of it.

Frequently M. Du Bos was invited to lecture away from the University. Once a friend ventured to explain that his audience would not be of college level intellectually. "In that case," answered M. Du Bos quickly, "I shall improvise. I can speak below my level. I cannot write below my level." Nothing so characterizes him as this devout Catholicity, this unfaltering honesty, "the spirit of sweet inflexibility," as Mauriac calls it. To have seen him assist at Mass, to have listened to him lecture, to have heard him intone the "Come, Holy Spirit," as he always did at the beginning of his classes, was to have entered with him deeply into the life of the spirit.

On the tenth of June 1939 he sailed for France on the *Normandie* with his wife and daughter. Madame Du Bos wrote from the boat and Primerose from Paris, reporting continuous illness during the trip. This was part of the chronic condition from which he had suffered for thirty years and which had been so acute in the spring as to prevent further writing or teaching. A letter from Primerose from La Celle St. Cloud dated August tenth reads:

"Father died last Saturday, the fifth, on the feast of Saint Mary of the Snow. He had the death he deserved, the death of a saint. He was quite conscious and asked himself for the sacraments. He had time to speak to each of us in particular, to tell us about his unfinished work. It was so great, so beautiful, that it gives courage to Mother and to me!"

It is impossible to measure the inheritance into which we have entered through the death of Charles Du Bos. The life that was light which he gave so lucidly under the veil of mortality now shines upon us through his participation in the beatific vision.

I come now from my digression, ending with the death of Charles Du Bos on August 5, 1939, to ourselves, Sister Verda Clare and me in Paris, 1933. On October 3, Madge called at our Paris convent to say goodbye. The feast of Saint Francis, October 4, brought me back to England. Lots of mail, a hot bath, a down quilt welcomed me at Cherwell Edge where the Sisters of the Holy Child mothered me for the year.

Matriculation at Oxford was a simple matter after the long waiting lines, the inquisitive registration cards, the involved choices attending one's induction to American University life. I registered for Father D'Arcy's lectures in philosophy at Baliol, Mr. Tolkein in fields of Old English. The friendships of these great scholars are now a part of life at Saint Mary's: Father D'Arcy as a most welcome guest, Mr. Tolkein in his absorbing romances.

More than anything or everything at Oxford, I awaited the wonder of the Bodleian library. Immediately after completing the paperwork and finances of entrance requirements I set out to that paradise of books. Following instructions, I entered an impressive archway which admitted me to a fair-sized court. A small door on the west wall of the court bore the unimpressive

legend, BODLEIAN LIBRARY. I walked over. This must be a back
entrance, a janitor's door. I did not even turn the knob. One
must enter the Bodleian by marble steps, bronze doors, age-old
architectural gateways. I walked out of the court and over to the
Camera. Here in its eighteenth century supplementary reading
room for the Bodleian are housed books more generally needed
by undergraduate students. But where was the Bodleian? I was
certain that I should know or find it by intuition. I went back to
the simple little door and its unobtrusive weathered sign. Still
I did not go in. The entrance was entirely too unimpressive. Back
at the convent, I asked again for directions. They brought me back
the next day to the same door. This time I opened it on to a dusty
wood stairway, dusty wood railing with, on the dusty landing,
Mother Margaret Williams, our dear little American Religious
of the Sacred Heart, and daughter of Michael Williams. She
greeted me with the enchantment of her hours among the
English word-hoards still upon her. 'Isn't the Bodleian wonderful?" she asked. I agreed completely!

My *Oxford University Handbook* had told me: "Each reader
will find his own experience the best guide." Again, I agreed.
Mine had begun. Cherwell Edge, my Oxford home, bordered
the river and walk to Mesopotamia. These were mine early
mornings, Addison's walk later in the day, and Chaucer's daisy
fields for longer jaunts. During the month flurries of American
guests called for tea, not fewer than seven on November 8. That
evening I met the Margaret Roper Club at 11 Norham Gardens,
the Convent of the Religious of the Sacred Heart.

The next morning I was awakened with a wire from Paris.
The second casualty determining the two major benedictions of
our year had occurred. Sister Verda Clare had had an emergency
appendectomy. I was in Paris that evening. Doctors insisted on
the Riviera for recuperation. We found the little town of Hyères,
twenty miles from Toulon, perfect for our needs, inexpensive
enough for our finances, with a convent on the Avenue des Iles

d'Or happy to receive us. Here Saint Louis landed on his return from the ninth crusade. Here Queen Victoria spent her winters year after year, and in La Solitude, his home on the mountain-side, Robert Louis Stevenson found the only happiness he knew in Europe.

We spent two heavenly months in Hyères. Edith Wharton lived almost beside us. Her magnificent library she made freely available. We sat out on her terrace at tea with the low Alps for our backdrop and the blue Mediterranean at our feet. We had the immortal experience of Christmas in Provence with its crèches, *santons,* midnight Mass, and the serenade music of the troubadours.

On January 26 we said reluctant goodbyes to our little family at the convent and our friends in the village. As a last-moment disclosure, some of the little old ladies at the pension revealed to us what to them was a great secret. They told us that they recognized the moment we entered the dining room that we were "chic." We asked them by what sign they knew this. They told us, half-fearful of shocking us, that we wore "high-heel shoes." This would be a mark of real style in a French nun.

Our itinerary to Rome provided stops at Cannes and Genoa. Arrived in Rome, we were met by three of our friends from Hyères who had gone on ahead of us. One of them is now a religious caring for the lepers in Madagascar.

XVI

Good Morning, Bishop

ONE single date we had set on the movable calendar of our year in Europe. We would begin the Holy Year novena in Rome at the Church of Saint Mary Major on February 2. In pouring rain, we crossed the city to Mass and Holy Communion. As we genuflected at the altar in Praesipio the celebrant turned and said, *Pax vobiscum.* I turned to my companions, saying, "I don't know what you want to do. I am staying here. This is Bishop Edwin O'Hara." We remained through his Mass. I followed him at a discreet distance to the door of the sacristy. As he came out, I said simply, "Good morning, Bishop."

The sequel is this: Archbishop Edward Howard, Bishop O'Hara, Father John Forest, O.F.M., Miriam Marks, Executive Secretary of the Confraternity of Christian Doctrine with her young niece, Miriam Marshall, were on pilgrimage to the Holy Land in the cause of the Confraternity New Testament then in preparation. As a gift and a compliment to the Sisters of the Holy Cross, we became honored and honorary pilgrims. We felt like co-tourists of Habecuc or Philip being carried off so marvelously to the good works of God.

Our week in Rome included an audience with our Holy Father, Pope Pius XI, in a party of perhaps twenty-five, visits to the churches of the pilgrimage, the greater galleries, Mass in the catacombs, a canonization at St. Peter's.

On February 9, we said goodbye to our dear friends from Hyères and were off to Naples. Here Mount Vesuvius floated its flag of smoke over an untidy city and an azure bay. Between blue skies and blue waters, we moved the next morning to the blue grottoes of Capri. Before ten the next morning we boarded the *Ausonia* for Alexandria. The Duke of Aosta was a passenger.

Landing at Alexandria amounted to major chaos. Tenders brought Arab porters aboard like ants. Wild confusion followed, mad scrambling for bags, disembarking amid frantic shouting, losing and finding luggage, tempestuous tips. Nothing we had ever known in American life could approximate it. Finally, and almost to our surprise, we found one another and all our worldly goods in the train for Cairo where we arrived for dinner.

February 14 was both the feast of Saint Valentine and Ash Wednesday. We received ashes at the Church of Saint Francis. Later, we visited the museum of King Tutankhamen, crossed the Nile on a hand-propelled barge to Pharaoh's Garden and the alleged bulrushes of Moses and on to the pyramids.

In the name of all incongruities we walked into a sightseeing party with the bill-boarded Josephine Baker, escorted by the city fathers of Cairo. We were mounted on camels and experienced the gentlest, most comfortable form of locomotion I had ever known. Each camel had a name. Mine was Kinstota, an Arabic word for "that I may drink." Symbolically, nothing could have more perfectly expressed my state of soul and expectant mind.

Traveling on ecclesiastical business, under the aegis of Saint Anthony and Father John, meant cars and Franciscan hospitality everywhere. Leaving Cairo for Jerusalem at 5:15 P.M. we were blocked by a sandstorm and a broken engine until after two in the morning. Good nature, good conversation, black Turkish coffee, well fortified, kept us half awake and less than half frozen. Lady Morgan, a beautiful English gentlewoman, had joined us. She and Archbishop Howard furnished the comic relief. We needed it. We crossed the Suez Canal at three in the morning, under the cold stars in a cold sky. The ferryboat across the canal was a barge primitive beyond belief. It did, however, span the narrow ribbon of water and land us into the turbulence of another customhouse. Fortunately, we had good compartments on a good train to Jerusalem.

Here spring comes in February. Wild tulips, anemone, cyclamen were in blossom. Children sold bunches at the station. We bought some, divided them among us, and entered the Holy City carrying flowers.

In Jerusalem we found Franciscan hospitality never more welcome. Day after day we assisted at Mass at the Church of the Holy Sepulcher, on Mount Calvary, at Gethsemane, at the Altar of the Annunciation in Nazareth. The Dead Sea proved more leaden than Great Salt Lake. Jericho confirmed every detail of its fall chronicled in the Book of Joshua. Our boat ride from Tiberias to Caphernaum and back violated all laws of navigation and human survival. Yet, we did survive.

Returning to Nazareth we drove west to Mount Carmel and its great monastery where seventeen languages are spoken and nineteen studied. Here we assisted at Mass in the cave of the Prophet Elias on Washington's Birthday. By train to Cairo, to Alexandria, and by boat back to Naples. The Mediterranean discouraged most of the passengers aboard our boat from dinner, and even breakfast. I thought of Aeneas and even of Saint Paul in perhaps not entirely different weathers. Sicily took on real local color as three itinerant violinists played "Santa Lucia" on our departure. To return to a city, even comparatively strange, gives one a sense of possession. My every entering through the gates of Rome made the city that much more my very own.

Term time in Oxford made stops in Assisi, Siena, Florence possible. Johannes Jörgensen had tea every afternoon at the Convent of the Franciscan Sisters of the Atonement where I stayed in Assisi. He bowed with old-world gallantry as we said goodbye. Saint Francis and Saint Clare became contemporary in his presence.

In Florence and in Siena, I left my heart, I think. If I never return to them I shall still never have left them wholly. Helen Robins, the sister-in-law of Joseph Pennell, was my friend and hostess in Siena. Her dining room, with its wainscoted frieze of Pennell etchings, made even her delicious food almost unessential. Her love of Saint Catherine and our pilgrimages to her home, her churches, made sanctity almost essential.

Milan meant chiefly the refectory housing the Last Supper of Leonardo da Vinci and Mass in the Chapel of Saint Charles Borromeo in the great sculptured-lace cathedral.

In Freiburg, the dear Dominican Sisters from Rosary College welcomed me to their home at Les Fougères. Two days were too brief but my Oxford leave of absence had become already overlong. I returned to Paris on Saint Patrick's day, leaving finally on Monday of Holy Week for Le Mans, Chartres and Solesmes. At Chartres, in care of Etienne Houvet, the dear father and custodian of the cathedral, I learned to read the texts of the great windows and to venerate with him the wonder of their beauty. Chartres is more than a name, more than a cathedral. It is a world, a life. If you have been there you know.

The rest of Holy Week I spent visiting with our Marianite Sisters in Le Mans, visiting the homes and the graves of our holy founders. On Holy Saturday I went to Solesmes, the great Benedictine capital of Gregorian Chant. The past months had given me canonization ceremonies, a papal audience, the Holy Land, and now Solesmes. If I had been there for the entire week I think I must have died of the sheer magnitude of the beauty that unfolded for me.

After Vespers and Compline, at the great gray monastic church on Holy Saturday, I walked down the dirt road under the quiet star-strewn sky to the little Villa Saint François, to think and to

dream until Easter dawn. At four in the morning I walked back
to the Church, in the light of the pale paschal moon for Matins
and Lauds and early Masses. After breakfast, I returned for
Prime, Tierce, Solemn Pontifical Mass, Sext and None, assisting with an expectant intensity and an attentive inner listening
to every chanted text, every sung note. This was the perfect
setting for the sacrifice of the Mass, almost too tremendous, too
beautiful to bear.

Returning to the Villa, I was conscious of a lovely fragrance
which led me to a wooded lane, carpeted with blue violets.
Here I sat, for hours I think, under a perfect sky, gathering them
and trying to grow up to the wonder of worship that I had lived
the past twenty-four hours. I returned to Paris that evening, my
small suitcase in one hand, violets in the other, and who can
say what memories in my heart? The next day I left for England
by way of Mont-Saint-Michel, Saint-Malo. The Sisters of Cavendish Square, London, and at Cherwell Edge, Oxford, amazed
at my Marco Polo adventures, asked, "Did nothing unpleasant
happen?" I said, "Nothing," and started back to school.

XVII

The Long Way Round

OXFORD that Trinity term meant and continues to mean for me Mr. C. S. Lewis. After attending his second lecture on the Prolegomena to the Study of Medieval Poetry I said to some of the students at Cherwell Edge, "Mr. Lewis is the one person at Oxford with whom I should like to tutor." "But," they exclaimed in amazement at my temerity, "Mr. Lewis refuses to tutor a woman." "That," I replied stoutly, "does not change my statement in the least."

You probably are not interested in a prolegomenon or preface to medieval poetry, or indeed in this archaic poetry itself. I should like, however, to share with you two experiences from the class in which Mr. Lewis dug up medieval poetry by the roots and planted it in our minds, there to grow and flower as it might. At the beginning of the course he announced by titles nineteen lectures. Later in the term he missed three of these because of illness. Returning to class, he stated that obviously some of the assigned lectures would have to be omitted. He asked that if we had any preference for those to be retained we would write him a note saying so. At Oxford, one does not stop a don before or after lectures for conference, or even for conversation. One writes him a note. The intercollege mail delivery among the colleges is the biggest and best form of communication and the accepted one at the University.

I had been anticipating impatiently the single lecture on Boethius. I wrote as much to Mr. Lewis. He gave in response three lectures on the author of *The Consolation of Philosophy*. This was the graciousness of the teacher.

Later, I wrote to thank him and to ask if there was available a bibliography on his course. He replied by writing out for me a history of the development of his study, a list of the books I should read relating to it, a list I might read, and a list to which I need pay no attention at all. This was the gentleman. Mr. Lewis had tutored me.

During term time I sat for an afternoon at the feet of Dean Inge as he lectured on "Liberty, Natural and Supernatural," asking such questions as "Why should the state be selected for apotheosis? It is the least inspiring of many national or international organizations to which we can belong." As he left the platform and the hall, unaccompanied, my inclination as an impulsive American was to go up and thank him for his talk. One does not do that at Oxford to a don, much less to a dean.

Another afternoon, Walter de la Mare talked on "Meanings of Words in Poetry." John Masefield sat directly in front of me in the hall. As the two walked out together after the lecture, my American impulse to hurry up to both in my enthusiasm for poets and poetry tugged at the bridle of English propriety. But I did walk close behind them all the way along the High to Magdalen Bridge.

Mrs. Michael Williams had been spending a part of the spring at Oxford where her daughter, Mother Williams, R.S.C., was studying. On June 3 we shared an intimation of Newman's Second Spring too long deferred. On that evening, the Sunday within the octave of Corpus Christi, an ancient glory returned to Oxford, England. The Blessed Sacrament was carried in procession in its streets for the first time in, perhaps, four hundred years. On the afternoon before, the ceremony of conferring university degrees had taken place in the old Sheldonian Theatre. There, in the name of the Father and of the Son and of the Holy Ghost, candidates were admitted to their academic honors according to the dignified Latin formula of the fifteenth century, from which all significance except that of antiquity seems to have fallen away. By contrast, the procession of the Blessed Sacrament, divinely vital for all its centuries of disuse, made its march of sacramental might from the Church of St. Aloysius to Blackfriars in a pageant that gathered a heroic past and future into its splendid present.

The great religious orders of men were there: Benedictines, Franciscans, Dominicans, Servites, Jesuits, Salesians; the religious orders of women: Sisters of the Holy Child, Mercy, Nazareth House, Holy Cross; the Oxford undergraduates in academic costume; the Sodalists; the children of the Catholic schools; the bodyguard of the Knights of St. Columba; the four Oxford professors in doctoral robes of crimson and scarlet and black, bearing the baldachin; the great congregation of the faithful. Like both pelican and phoenix the beautiful living body rose, one might think, from the blood and ashes of the past.

Perennial youth marked its progress from altar to altar. Down Woodstock Road, peopled with a thousand memories, it walked with God that late afternoon, past St. Giles's Church, that seven hundred years ago raised the lancet-lighted tower from which bells sweeten the air of Oxford still; past St. Benet's Hall, the Benedictine place of peace and study; past Pusey House, the heart of a high and earnest Anglo-Catholicism; past the Jesuit house of studies, Campion Hall; by all that's in a name, the Blackfriars, where this second time the sons of Saint Dominic have returned to the seat of wisdom for which they had laid the stone of the corner. There opposite the severely beautiful front of St. John's College, the long procession stopped for Benediction in the fine chapel of Blackfriars. Then the singing progress took its way back to the Church of St. Aloysius where, with a second Benediction, this most significant pilgrimage to honor the Blessed Sacrament ended. Among those officiating were the flower of the priesthood in England today, Fathers Carpenter and D'Arcy, Monsignor Ronald Knox. And who shall forbid the spirit of Newman that paradisal walk in the evening air of his Oxford!

Among academic events of the year, encaenia takes precedence. According to the order of proceedings,

"The doors of the Theatre will open at a QUARTER PAST ELEVEN O'CLOCK. . . .

"The Burgesses, Proctors, Heads of Houses, and Doctors of Divinity, Civil Law, Medicine, Music, Letters, and Science, invited to partake of Lord Crewe's Benefaction to the University, meet the Chancellor in the Hall of Worcester College, at twenty minutes past Eleven o'clock; whence they go in procession to the Theatre.

"THE PROCESSION enters the Theatre at TWELVE O'CLOCK precisely."

The date was June 20. The procession, reaching from the westernmost college of Oxford to its very heart, the Sheldonian Theatre, moved in the pageantry of letters, arts, sciences as old as the University itself and reflecting in color and design the enthronement of the intellectual life in its proper city, its acknowledged capital. Along George Street they came, along the Broad, to the Theatre's gates: Bachelors in cap and fur-bordered hood and gown; Masters, black-gowned, with crimson hoods; Doctors, resplendent in crimson-hooded black gown with sleeves of crimson silk or French gray. Silk braided broadcloth with full-crowned hats marched beside taffeta rose and cream brocades. Black velvet beside blue, gray with white until at twelve o'clock precisely the procession entered the Theatre. Here indeed the philosophy of clothes found complete fulfillment, once quaintly described by Carlyle's German professor: "From the soberest drab

to the high flaming scarlet, spiritual idiosyncrasies unfolded themselves in the choice of color; if the cut betoken intellect and
talent, so does the color betoken temper and heart."

The Chancellor opened the convocation immediately, an-
nouncing and conferring "HONORARY DEGREES . . . on certain
distinguished persons." André Maurois was among these. Then
followed the CREWEIAN ORATION, the prizes for English, Greek,
Latin verse and prose, after which, as announced by the great
staid program, "THE CHANCELLOR dissolved the CONVOCATION."

My valedictory had not been announced, but this was it. On
July 1, I left Oxford, detached it is true, but never, never pulled
up by the roots.

XVIII

47 Palace Court

ONCE during term time I went through the Cotswolds with an American friend, returning by way of Stratford for a matinee performance of *Henry V*. British English may not trouble other Americans. It did confuse me. But at the Shakespeare Memorial Theatre I heard the English that I knew, spoken as I had sometimes heard it in the United States and as I myself try to speak it. I submit this as a fact, not as a compliment. Our American speech habits are far from meriting that.

On a weekend in April I went down to London for an appointment at 47 Palace Court. Monica Lucas, an elder daughter of Wilfrid Meynell, greeted me at the door. As I entered the magical library her father said, by way of introduction and welcome, "Sister, I have made one mistake in my life." "What is that?" I asked in surprise. "I have had my eighty-first birthday." After that we were not only acquainted, we were friends.

Seated with him before an open fire, I listened to wonder stories of Francis Thompson, his beloved Alice, Dicky Doyle who designed the cover still used on *Punch*, Coventry Patmore, George Meredith, the Brownings. "Just there on the rug before the fire, Francis Thompson used to lie and play with the children or dream in the firelight. Alice sat at the table here, wrote 'The

Shepherdess,' and gave it to me to read before the ink was dry on it. As I read it I said, 'This, I think, may be the poem by which you will be best remembered.' "

I agreed with him. Then he went on, "I was in a bookstore the other day making some purchases. As I gave the attendant my name she asked, 'Not by any chance a relative of Alice Meynell?' 'Her husband,' I said proudly. Then she quoted:

'She walks—the lady of my delight—
A shepherdess of sheep.'

'Ten thousand shop girls in London, Mr. Meynell, bless your wife for writing those lines.' "

The afternoon was one of pure enchantment. Manners rather than desire forced me to say at last that I must go. The taxi came. Mr. Meynell took me to the door, to the cab, and waved farewell. I drove off, feeling like a little girl of five saying goodbye to a fairy godfather. There must be at least one such person in the world. I had spent the afternoon with him.

A number of times Hilary Pepler had come to visit me at Cavendish Square, London, and in Oxford. We were both absorbed in the liturgy, mimes, the restoration of the medieval arts and crafts. With Father Vincent McNabb, O.P., and Eric Gill he had laid the foundations for a religious art center at Ditchling. Conrad, his son and a Dominican scholastic at Black-friars, Oxford, occasionally visited with me at Cherwell Edge. It is pleasant to remember Father Conrad Pepler, O.P., the editor of *Black Friars* and *The Sword of the Spirit* in these untroubled student days.

His father and sister Susan came up in June to fetch me for a weekend with the Meynells at Greatham, Sussex, their country home. Such a Utopia! How shall I tell of it: A great seventeenth century stone and beam house, set well back from a brick and rock wall, with poplar trees named for the twelve apostles between; rooms with whitewashed walls and natural wood beams and timbered gable, patchwork quilted beds, antique chairs and chests. All said "seventeenth century" to me. But they said even more certainly, "This is Alice Meynell's home."

Alice had been with God for a decade or more, but from Greatham she was never absent. The great living room library had been built for her in 1907, walled with books by and for her as the years brought them. Bookshelves under the windows were piled with files of magazines. Wilfrid opened one to a contemporary criticism of a poem by Browning. Against it in the margin, Robert had written in bold, indignant script, "This is a lie!"

It would be easier to say what one could not than what one could find on the shelves, the tables, the desks, in the copious graciousness of this room: first editions, limited, rare editions, inscribed, autographed volumes, books out of print, piles of letters from poets, critics, writers from everywhere and on everything. Walking about from shelf to shelf with me, taking down special treasures here and there, Wilfrid said, "Take anything you want in this room, Sister." It was like saying, in the vernacular, "All this and heaven, too!"

Viola Meynell Dallyn was our hostess. Her sister Monica lived in one of the smaller houses provided for the family. Shane Leslie, not yet knighted, shared with us the incomparable Meynell hospitality. After dinner, we sat around the great open fire, reading aloud, chiefly from Francis Thompson, and talking of the world of writers for whom the editor of *Merrie England* and Alice had been angels. After such an evening, what more could one dream of the night long?

We went to Mass at Storrington in the morning and back to breakfast, where our fruit was gooseberry fool. Though I knew it only as a name I recognized it at sight, much to my own satisfaction since Mr. Meynell challenged me on it. At table, I sat directly in front of a wide, low fireplace. After breakfast we looked up the lefthand side of this chimney. Here, about five feet up, was a substantial shelf, a priests' hiding hole from Reformation days. We were brought close to the frightening realities of persecution as we ourselves stood where who can say how many a hunted priest had stood and stepped to safety beside and above the flames and smoke of a blazing fireplace!

By contrast, we found at the out-of-door swimming pool a fine statue of Christ from a seventeenth century Spanish group portraying His baptism. Mr. Meynell remarked more than once that the face of Christ looked much like George Meredith when he was talking with Alice. It pleased me to add this to my memories of that Platonic friendship, his Dear Portia letters to her and his violets buried with her.

Parting from Greatham was in unwonted ways "such sweet sorrow." After repeated goodbyes, we left for tea at the home of Hilaire Belloc on our way to Ditchling. He had gone across country that afternoon, but the brilliant conversation of his daughter Elizabeth provided gracious hospitality. Saint Dominic's Press, the oldest hand press in England; the chapel furnished with handwoven vestments; studios for arts and crafts in metals, ivory, wood; fields for agriculture, "the long line of the downs," English skylarks—all these we met at Ditchling, a weekend to exceed all weekends and my last before leaving Oxford.

XIX

The Best Way Home

MY LUGGAGE for the year, my typewriter, my book box and I rang the doorbell at Cavendish Square for my last sojourn there on July 1. What a convent for a home, and what a home for memories! A block north of Oxford Street and Oxford Circus, the American Embassy on the opposite corner to my left, Wimpole Street and the home of the Barretts to the right, down Marylebone, straight ahead two blocks to the cloistered Dominican convent, built on the site of Tyburn, sanctified by the seventeenth century maniac hangings of priests and layfolk. All this was our environment, with Hyde Park and the Marble Arch a pleasant evening's walk beyond. These were our afterdinner recreations during my last week in London.

On July 8, Julie Kernan and I took part in a small pilgrimage from Chelsea down the Thames to the Tower to honor the fourth centenary of the execution of Saint Thomas More. Past the grim Traitors' Gate we went to the boat landing, then through the gray corridors of the Tower to the room where the King's Good Servant looked out of a slot of a prison window to the boundless freedoms of eternity and wrote with a charred coal that last poignant letter to his good daughter Margaret with its tender comment, "I have never liked your manner toward me better than when you kissed me last." And still on to the gray stone house where royal prisoners, looking out on to the court and the site of the scaffold could watch the executions of companions in royal disfavor while waiting for their own. Their names, and sometimes brief commentaries scratched on the walls told a cryptic story of their rendezvous with death. Our last tribute to Saint Thomas More we paid with Benediction of the Blessed Sacrament at the Church of the English Martyrs.

This chronicle I find is becoming more and more a business of what to leave out. But this you must know. At the very last weekend in London I went down to meet Frank Sheed and Frederick Page on Pater Noster Row, Ave Maria Lane, Amen Corner. Where in all the world could I have matched this journey's end? Nowhere else then, and nowhere now. Bombs have torn all this out of the heart of London.

By the happiest circumstances I spent my last Sunday with May Lamberton Becker and her daughter, Beatrice Warde, a distinguished calligrapher and typographer. We had met at the British Museum the day before, quite by chance. Our friendships, enthusiasms, and Americanism carried over through the Sunday afternoon at the Tate Gallery, with William Blake chiefly, then to dinner and reluctant farewells.

One may visit the English Cathedral towns in many ways. For me, my way will always be the best. On the seventeenth of July, Hilary Pepler, Susan and I drove to Cambridge where the Tudor Chapel clothed us in splendor and gracious English nuns gave us hospitality; then through the charm of the English countryside, its ubiquitous windmills under Wedgwood sky to Ely, on impatiently to Norwich, where even more than the Cathedral, the fieldstone Church and shrine of Dame Julian awaited us. Susan's friend, Ruth, joined us here as we drove North through poppy fields to the Church, shrine and convent of Our Lady of Walsingham, now reverently kept by Anglican nuns. After one more stop at Boston we reached Lincoln for the night. We came into the

Cathedral just at Evensong with its boy choir singing, "Jesus joy of man's desiring." The text always true in its Bach setting and its 'litel clergeons' there and then could hardly have been lovelier.

York was one of our objectives. We had come in part on pilgrimage to Blessed Margaret Clitherow whose shrine is at the Bar Convent. If this were a book on English Cathedral towns, I should never finish even one of them, York least of all. Happily, we spent the feast of Saint Mary Magdalen, my patron, there, between the Cathedral with the ruby-jeweled gray Five Sisters windows and the great Roman city walls. Here Mr. Pepler left us and his son Mark took on the driving and the second part of our journey.

Presently we were on our way to Whitby, the fishing village, the grave of Caedmon, the double monastery of Saint Hilda, still majestic in its unprotesting ruins. A hundred feet below, the restive North Sea across which she looked toward her dreamed-of Norman world still matched its futile strength against the black stone promontory.

In the past four months I had knelt at the shrines of my predilect friends: Saint Francis of Assisi, Dame Julian of Norwich, and now Saint Hilda. And on a day in Hyères we had driven over to *La Sainte Baume*, the immense grotto in which legend says that Saint Mary Magdalen lived in solitude and prayer until her death. We had of course gone to Bethany and Magdala in Palestine. A thousand dollars had brought me many riches beyond Oxford.

From Whitby Mark drove us west to Haworth where we arrived in late afternoon. We stopped at a shop for tea, bought a loaf of whole-wheat bread, a pound of butter, as much of cheese, a bag of sweet biscuits, and a butcher knife. Again we stopped to engage lodgings for the night, then drove up into the moors, parked the car and found ourselves heather seats among the rocks. In good American style, I cut, buttered, and cheesed the bread into sandwiches. We ate and talked on many of the burning subjects of the day, among them the barrier which the religious habit imposes on social relations with the secular world. My young English trio were strong for defrocking us all. I looked at my watch. I looked at the twilight western sky. In this latitude darkness scarcely comes until midnight. It was ten o'clock. Remembering our early morning start next day, I took over brushing the crumbs away and getting back to our car and our lodgings for bed and breakfast. In the process, we all had a good laugh at our conversation so gaily uninhibited by one religious habit of a Sister of the Holy Cross.

After breakfast, we visited the parsonage home of the Brontës, the cemetery, and the somber environment in which *Jane Eyre* and *Wuthering Heights* had had their inceptions.

Chester we reached that afternoon, visited its red sandstone Cathedral, walked on the city walls and on the rows, the double lines of main streets with covered second stories. We remembered that this ancient military *castrum* is the one city in England which never gave up its Catholic faith.

It would seem that in all this Cathedral pilgrimage we neither slept nor ate. There were hospitable convents, cheery inns. We stayed at both. We lunched and dined at such beguiling dining rooms as the Crown, the Queen, Magpie Inn, Rope and Anchor, and with the good Ursuline Sisters at the Dee House, Chester.

Time had come for another valedictory. Mark, Susan and Ruth returned to London, leaving me to a pleasant train ride to Holyhead, a choppy hour across the Irish Sea and the *summum bonum,* Dublin at its end.

XX

From Dublin to Donegal

AT OXFORD I had asked, simply, if I might possibly meet Father Ronald Knox. I had been charged to do this by my good mutual American friends. But the conservative English sisters discouraged me; Father Knox was not easily accessible, they implied, and I remained discouraged. Imagine my amusement when one day on the Riviera I received a letter addressed in red ink to:

> Sister Mary Madeleva of the Rocky Mountains
> In care of Father Ronald Knox
> Oxford, England

and readdressed by the reputedly inaccessible Father to me at my convent home in Hyères. The mountain, it seemed, had come to Mohammed.

The letter was from my devoted friend, Seumas MacManus, the poet and shanachie, importuning me not to return to America without accepting his hospitality in Ireland. But who would!

Sunday in Dublin I spent with the Yeatses at Rothfarnham, with "Willie," his kindly wife, his robust daughter. Tea and cakes, a walk in the garden prefaced our real visit in his library where the great-hearted, white-haired Irish poet, without his greater birthright of faith, talked with me. He read to me from his own poems and from those of that kindred Gaelic muse, Ella Young.

No one but Seumas MacManus could have revealed to me the Ireland that I saw under his enchanting courtesies. First, he arranged for me to go to Lough Dergh, Saint Patrick's Purgatory, without complying with a single rule for setting foot on this place of austere pilgrimage. Hundreds go barefooted and fasting to the Island for three days of vigil, black fast and prayer. A great boat with two stout oarsmen waited for me at the landing on my arrival. They rowed against a bitter wind which did everything to my cap and veil short of blowing them off my head. Once on the Island I was welcomed by the Canon. Later, I joined the praying pilgrims, stopping at the beds of Saint Patrick and Saint Brigid and the great Basilica, the central places of devotion. Mr. MacManus and his friends were waiting to drive me a short fifteen miles to Mount Charles, his home in Donegal. Here, with his cousin Mrs. Tierney as my hostess and her home my home, I spent ten days in sheer Gaelic enchantment.

The town itself is a bit of a village, of one street, climbing up the hillside where on this charmed week the tinkers were camping. At the top of the hill, looking into four counties, and the trysting place of more of the "good people" than are in all the island, Mr. MacManus had a pretty, pleasant home. Here, I think, his daughters and his good friend, Percy MacKaye, may have stayed during their summers in Ireland. Seumas himself lived in a fine substantial house opposite the Tierneys.

Every day brought its unique adventure. We began with Mass and a visit to the grave of Ethna Carberry, the gifted poet-wife of Seumas, who died with and at the birth of their child. Later we drove up to the fishermen's cottages on the rugged Atlantic coast, the country about which Peader O'Donnell wrote, "The Way It Was with Them." Here, in the whitewashed, brown-timbered cottages with their heavy thatched roofs, I saw just that. Through the wide, low chimneys we could look up at the clear

blue sky and the soft blue peat smoke rising to meet it from the
turf fire. The kitchen dresser with its literal sideboard of brown-
figured or bright-colored cups, saucers, plates, the outshot bed by
the fireplace, the wag-by-the-wall long pendulumed clock, the
Saint Brigid's crosses tucked up among the rafters, the half-lofts
—all became part of my home economics in Donegal. I was glad
to have my first lessons in the cottages of fishermen. Thousands of
sardine-sized fish shone silver in baskets on the rocks outside
their doors. We came past rivers, atumble with waterfalls, to
Lock Esk, lying north and south among mountains with coves,
wooded shores, "the white-beached lake of the mouth of pearls."
A man in a hayfield came up to the fence and told us a story in
Gaelic. Seumas matched it with the story of "The woman of three
white cows" and its burthen, "As you are strong, be merciful."
Here I was, among the singers and bards, children of the epic
poets of the past, in a company and an art rare and all but lost in
our Western world.

All the way back to the village, Seumas half-chanted tales
from Fioin who had the thumb of wisdom which he got from the
salmon of wisdom, then the three burthens of the Wife of *the*
O'Donnell. The village children, hearing the chug of his precarious car, ran out to meet and hail him. They greeted us half-
shyly. Upon our eager request, they buoyantly found themselves
in reels and slip jigs, hands and arms motionless, free knees,
ankles and toes, heads splendidly erect. All this they matched
with Gaelic songs and their moving minor refrains like a cry.
Every day began with Mass. Every day was rich with the lived
life of an enchanting and partly enchanted people. The morning
at the home of James McCahill may stand as one for all. Mr.
McCahill was ninety-two. He sat erect in his rocking chair by
the fireplace, one arthritic leg crossed over his good knee, a white
knitted shawl around his shoulders. Standing, he could have been
well over six feet. His profile could have been carved on a
cameo or a Roman coin. He wore no glasses on his keen, dark

eyes, an unmistakable mark of Spanish heritage. I need hardly say that the beads of his fifteen-decade rosary were slipping through his long, slender fingers.

He greeted me, proud to hold the hand of a sister, and hoped that it would cure his bad foot. He sang for me "The Song of the Green Broom" and another celebrating the prowess of "Bony," Napoleon Bonaparte, whose virtue consisted in a dislike of Cromwell. To the innumerable stanzas of this song he improvised an additional one in honor of the sister from America. He asked me to pray God to give him a happy death, named the four men he had already appointed "to carry his bones out of the house." Two others he had chosen to forbid men he had listed from coming to his wake. These were the misguided countrymen who had failed to support de Valera. Never have I met a gayer spirit. What a great half hour it had been! We said goodbye chuckling at the implications of his daughter's parting comment, "Too much religion can put you wrong."

The Tighes were friends of the MacManuses as who were not? We stopped a moment to see them. The household was all aflurry! A trunk from America had come the day before. The girls had been better than busy far into the night and all morning, trying on dresses and shoes.

The First Friday of August was my last day in Donegal. After Mass we drove to Bundoran, Seumas chanting songs and folk-lore all the way. Mrs. Tierney bade me goodbye as a mother might have done. Mr. MacManus, the absolutely perfect host, bought my ticket, the only first-class railway passage I had had in Europe.

Presently I was in Galway! I was leaving Ireland. No, I had not seen the Lakes of Killarney; no, I had not kissed the Blarney stone; no, I had not ridden in a jaunting car. But I had seen Ireland from Dublin to Donegal, from William Butler Yeats to Seumas MacManus. I had ridden through miles of fuchsia hedge, had stood among blossoming foxglove as tall as myself, had been on the moors in the long twilight of the unending summer evenings with the "good people" all about me. I had known and lived with and shared deeply the world, the culture, the spontaneous hospitality, the indigenous charm of a people that I love.

XXI

Taking the Blame for Things

I LEFT Europe reluctantly, sailing from Galway, the very last port of call for boats to America. My final forty-eight hours were part Saturday, part a rainy, turbulent Sunday, and, for comic relief, the last days of the races. All day long hundreds of white swans flew, crying from the river to the bay, from the bay to the river. I had never known that there were so many swans in the world. Winter that year brought us a strange, restless snowstorm with winds blowing and crying across the campus. For me the swans of Galway had returned. I wrote this much in a brief lyric, "Snowstorm." The World's Fair in New York City gave it first place among poems from Indiana. By birth, a loyal Wisconsin Badger, by transplanting a Utah Beehiver, I was now qualified as an Indiana Hoosier poet.

Our boat stopped at Boston. I disembarked, took the New York Central west and was in South Bend before my good ship *Scythia* had come to port in New York City. This was August 13. On the fifteenth I received my obedience—the religious idiom for assignment or job—as president of Saint Mary's College. The one position which our Superior General, Mother Vincentia, had repeatedly assured me would not be assigned to me she had appointed me to fill.

Once, in crossing by boat from Buffalo to Detroit, I overheard this conversation just outside my cabin:

Wife: Who runs this boat?
Husband: The captain.
Wife: What does he do?
Husband: Nothing.
Wife: Oh! but he must do something.
Husband: No, he doesn't. He doesn't do a thing.
Wife: Who does the work?
Husband: The crew. You'll see. The crew does the work. He sits in his office. He doesn't do anything.
Wife: (still unconvinced) Well, I suppose there has to be someone to take the blame for things.

In parable, this is my story for the past twenty-five years—taking the blame for things. I came to Saint Mary's College at the all-low ebb of the depression, 1934. We had an enrollment of just under three hundred, a magnificent new Tudor Gothic residence hall, dining room and classroom building, a debt of a million dollars. I had left Salt Lake City with a debt approximating that, so the business of paying interest was fairly familiar, however irksome. Here, I found myself responsible for a school ninety years old, a great heritage, a developing plant, a magnificent campus, potentials in faculty and students to dream of and to work with. The best qualifications I brought to my office were these: my ability to dream, my capacities to work.

During my first two years in administration, not knowing what better to do, I taught two courses: one in writing, one in literary criticism. I knew every student by name. I looked around a bit. I thought. The Catholic University invited me to teach two graduate summer courses. I accepted and am still grateful for the friendships they occasioned. Dom Verner Moore was a great spiritual oasis. With Sister Olivia, O.S.B., Sister Amadeo and I began plans for our present department of nursing education.

Gradually, I began to see light. First things must come first. The chapel of the Holy Spirit in Le Mans Hall had been reserved almost entirely for the students. The sisters went to the Church of Our Lady of Loretto for all their religious exercises. Remembering that our Lady is the mediatrix of all grace, we asked and were granted permission to chant her office three times a day in the chapel of the Holy Spirit. For years, members of our own lay faculty and students joined us. Their own spiritual exercises have now replaced ours for them.

Under the direction of Father William Cunningham, C.S.C., we rewrote our college bulletin, reorganizing it under the four basic areas of educational development: physical, intellectual, spiritual, social. The job was pretty thoroughgoing. Although it has been done twice since, the changes have been largely matters of rearrangement.

The revised bulletin made a complete dichotomy of the curriculum into upper and lower division courses. This obviated the *mélange* of students from freshmen to seniors in the same classes. The new bulletin provided for senior comprehensive examinations as the final academic hurdle before the Bachelor's degree.

In December of the first year, the dean of women developed an ulcer that perforated. Before the third week of January she was hurried to the hospital for an emergency appendectomy. At midnight, three days later, her assistant woke me with, "I feel like a horse thief to bother you, but I am as sick as I can be." Our doctor came posthaste. We bundled Sister into his car and drove her to the hospital for the second emergency operation in three days. If asked the score at that dark moment, I could have said: "Two down and a whole semester to go!"

With these inauspicious precedents, Sister Maria Pieta undertook the work of dean of women. Our dean of studies attended the National Convention of the Association of American Colleges that year with me at Atlanta, Georgia. There we met Dr. Eugenie Leonard, dean of women at Syracuse, through whom Julie Read, one of her graduates, came to us as our first lay assistant dean of women. We could not have been more fortunate.

Great teachers are the first requisite for a good school. We set about following Mother Pauline's sustained precedent of finding them, making them, and keeping them. Two of our youngest sisters were completing training in library science at Saint Catherine's College, St. Paul. A third was at the Art Institute in Chicago. Candidates for Doctors' degrees in English and German were at work at the University of Notre Dame and the Catholic University. This was the *status quo* in 1934. Since that time, the Sisters of the Holy Cross on our faculty have qualified for Doctors' degrees at the Catholic University, Columbia, Harvard, Laval, University of Notre Dame, Yale, and in our own School of Sacred Theology. Many have earned their Masters' degrees from graduate schools in their particular fields. The process goes on. This, I hope, is only a report of progress. Academic processions, Honors convocations, participation in professional conferences, conventions, and societies are all a part of it. Changes like growth occur so unobtrusively that we are unaware of them until we look back across the decades.

A good school needs good students. What makes a student good? "Responsibility," I depose. Let transcripts tell the story proper to them. Working with a comparatively small student body, less than three hundred, we set up officers and an organization for such student government as the girls themselves were willing to undertake. Today one finds it strange that they had to have this form of student life almost thrust upon them. Frankly, they did not want to take the blame for things. Through the processes of normal, thoughtful, well-directed growth, the student body today is capable and responsible for undertaking wise and constructive judgments and procedures for its thousand and more members.

In 1934 Lady Nicotine had none but a surreptitious place in Catholic colleges for women. The childishness and dishonesty of our solution to the problem of smoking on campus affronted me. With the approval of every parent, save one, we opened our recreation rooms to smoking. The long lines and queues of secret smokers to the attics of our dormitories and the boathouse on the campus were ended. Some of us denounced the procedure as the breaking down of the sacrosanct tradition and respectability of Saint Mary's until we made our summer visits to our own homes and found them in soft hazes of cigarette smoke. That taught us tolerance and better judgment.

Saturday and Sunday afternoons, chairs in the social hall were pushed back and the famous tea dances of the thirties and forties became the prevailing social mood from three to five. Occasionally, a detached boy drifted into my office. These campus nephews liked to talk to someone for whom they would not have eventually to buy a steak dinner. Young Tom Dooley, a premedical student and a gifted musician, came often. Sitting at the piano for much of the afternoon and playing for the other boys and girls to dance, he would find himself at the end of ends without a companion. I was not much compensation for his generosity in playing for an afternoon of dancing. Still, I think he did not mind too much. He was trying at the time to decide whether to become a doctor or a concert pianist. He needed to get all the reasons out in the open. He left college for medical school and from there went into service.

Two years ago, on a summer afternoon, I heard the piano in our lounge speaking the musical language of only one person I knew. I went in. Tom Dooley was playing. I couldn't have mistaken it. He was just back from Viet-Nam—the chronicler of his own Christlike service there under the title, *Forgive Us Our Trespasses*. Released from service, Dr. Dooley returned to practice medicine in Laos, the northernmost accessible part of Indochina. This man is a Samaritan. He came back to the United

States early in 1958, with the manuscript of his second book, *The Edge of Tomorrow*, now between boards, and his irresistible appeal for the most Christlike help. The dozens of young doctors, the scores of nurses and other helpers, the thousands of dollars worth of medication and equipment that have met his appeal provide a great commentary on the alleged materialism of our time. We have not been asked to do things hard enough for us.

When we discarded tablecloths in our refectory we feared that we had lost our last claim to gentility. When we changed the hour for dinner from noon to night we hoped that we had reclaimed it somewhat. When we set up our staff student service program in the dining room we were certain, and we still are, that we offer in it the best opportunity for student self-help on any campus today. Built like, but preceding the program of nurses' service in operation during the war, it enables students to complete their college in five years or less, being completely self-supporting, even to incidentals, and free of student loans.

We are among the few boarding schools maintaining family service for all our meals. The Saga Food Service provides this on the level of a fine art. This we have installed during the past two years. Our three meals a day at which we all gather as a family we consider our biggest and our best course in Western civilization.

An even better precedent we set for all civilization in 1941. At the Liturgical Conference held in Saint Meinrad's, Indiana, that year, Monsignor Morrison met me in the corridor with the abrupt, "Sister, will you accept Negro students at Saint Mary's?" For years I had been waiting for this question. I knew only one answer, the right one. If it emptied the school, we would enroll Negro girls in residence. My answer to Monsignor was simply, "Yes, Monsignor, we will." "Good," he said, "I'll send you a dandy." That ended discussion of race problem as a school policy, but not repercussions! Southern parents wrote enraged letters telling me that as a Northerner I did not know what I was

doing. I answered that, however conditioned by my own upbringing, I was acting under the direction of Cardinal, then
Archbishop, Stritch who had been born and reared in Memphis.
A round robin of protest went to him. He sent me a copy of his
reply, with the reassurance, "You are right, Sister. Stick to your
guns!"

Carmelita Desobrey, a beautiful Creole girl, came to Saint
Mary's in September. By the third semester she led the school
academically. She stood first on the Honor Roll, with a major in
science.

XXII

Concrete and Catwalks

SISTER LAURITA and I were walking across the campus one spring morning in 1937.

"We never get anything for the home economics department," she said, by way of information.

"What do you need?" I asked.

"A model practice house," she answered.

"Have you ever asked for one?"

"No," she said, thinking such a request futile.

"Suppose you ask," I suggested.

She did, and so did I. Charles Riedinger and his sister Caroline had given us five thousand dollars in memory of the fiftieth and twenty-fifth graduations of their mother and their sister. On this foundation the Riedinger house was built. Blessed and dedicated on June 11, 1939, it has been a house, a home, a school for all home economics majors since. They are asking now for newer and better food and clothes construction laboratories. We are listening.

At Saint Mary's for a brief two weeks in the summer of 1925, I ran again and again along the catwalks in Le Mans Hall, then in concrete forms. Intuitively, I found the area designed for the library. It was planned chiefly as two beautiful reading rooms with adjoining offices. A library proper was contemplated for some future time. But when? Why need libraries break one's heart? I tried to apply the sedation, "It isn't my problem." That was more than ten years earlier. Now it had become my problem.

Every possibility had been exhausted to make possible what had been from the first an impossible situation. I have told students plenty of times that we can have anything we want if we want it badly enough. We wanted a new library just that badly.

Mrs. Anna White Rempe loved Saint Mary's to the extent of sending her seven daughters here to high school and college. She invited us up to Chicago for luncheon on a day and with the Victorian formalities of candles and flawless service, in the presence of her three sons and her seven daughters, she gave us a check for twenty-five thousand dollars. This built the Anna White Rempe room in our new library. A bequest from the Breen family, friends of the Sisters of the Holy Cross from Fort Wayne, added forty-one thousand dollars. Our alumnae turned mendicants for the rest. Frances Lyons, Helen Holland Voll, and Marie Broussard Weir set up an office on the campus.

Our community was to celebrate the centenary of its founding in 1941. This centenary formed the commencement theme. Ground-breaking for the Alumnae Centennial Library was for us the major event. Five minutes later would have been too late. Suddenly, we were in war. The library was the last major building done in this area for the duration. Bishop Noll laid the cornerstone amid torrential rain.

Even when I came as a student to Saint Mary's in 1906 the sisters were talking of an auditorium. Anyone knowing Saint Angela's, our hybrid Exhibition Hall, will understand why. By the 1940's classes had begun to speculate on which would be the first to graduate from this mythical new building. Meanwhile, the art department had been persuaded to exchange their dubious two rooms in Holy Cross for the very attractive and larger area vacated by the library. By what I facetiously call the triumph of the Teutonic mind, we metamorphosed the place into studios, workrooms, display areas, without pounding a nail.

But we were only temporizing. Our growing community had absorbed old classrooms and much of the music hall. A new convent now in blueprint took the right-of-way over what was left. On Easter Sunday, 1952, Sister Mary Agnes, our superior, and I went over to the administration building to greet our superior general, Mother Rose Elizabeth. She stood on the porch and pointed to the demolition entailed by the new construction.

"What shall we do for a music hall?" I asked, as I added one more to her many problems.

"Build your fine arts building," was Mother's reply.

For ten years we had considered and rejected plans for this will-o'-the-wisp. Five years earlier Mother assured me that she did not believe that I could undertake it. This I had considered final and had stopped thinking about the matter. Mother herself provided new curtains and drapes for Saint Angela's Hall. We cleaned up the beautiful, mellowed old wood. Today was Easter. The fine arts building was about to arise from our dead hope.

Astounded at Mother's ultimatum, I stammered, "When?"

"Now," she answered promptly.

"Now is tomorrow and I am going to Des Moines. Shall I stop in Chicago to find an architect?" I asked inclusively.

"Yes, do!" in her most benign manner.

Noah was a hundred years old when God set him to building the Ark. God willed the Ark. John the Baptist was born to Zachary and Elizabeth when they were well past their youth. God wished John. Perhaps He wished the fine arts building. Intoxicating possibility! Only under such recurrent intoxications did it come to be.

Sister Francis Jerome had been for the fifty years of her community life one of our best loved sisters. For years before my return to Saint Mary's as president and until her death in 1948, she was vice-president: kindly, tolerant, patient with me in all my wild extremes. At her death she left by will close to half a million dollars, her portion of a family inheritance. This, her will specified, should be used for a fine arts building.

Her brother John became increasingly impatient to see this building in blueprint and in brick and concrete. On our return from Des Moines he met and took us to his friend, Charlie Murphy of Naess and Murphy, Architects. Within a fortnight, Mr. Murphy and three of his company met with our superiors in my office. They were authorized to begin studies for a fine arts building to include an auditorium for about a million dollars.

Meanwhile, we had gone through the experience of organizing a board of lay trustees and had had at least three semiannual meetings. Meanwhile, also, as an act of God, a fire from spontaneous combustion, so we still believe, broke out in one of our science laboratories. Our entire science department was housed in the front of our freshman residence hall. The damage was not great and was well covered by insurance. But the trustees insisted that a science hall take priority over any other possible building.

Tom Mulig of Naess and Murphy was interrupted in his dream and made a blueprint for a fine, sturdy, adequate science hall, costing something over half a million. The cornerstone was laid in bitter wind and rain. The building went into service the second semester of 1954.

Again, blueprints for the fine arts building were labored over. At their completion, on July 22, 1954, we encountered our last delay. The architects, with admirable patience, waited. In December we were instructed to go ahead.

On January 12, 1955, bids were let and on February 26, 1955, ground was broken. Again, it rained. Responding to Mr. Murphy's review of plans and purposes at the program of the day, I said that our auditorium was moving from myth to mud and that our buildings, planted in the rain, had flourished and borne rich fruit. This continues to be true.

Of none is it more true than of Moreau Hall, the name chosen
for the entire center. Appropriately, the auditorium is called by
the family name of Sister Francis Jerome, O'Laughlin Auditorium. Years ago, Eric Gill wrote, "Take care of goodness and
truth, and beauty will take care of herself." I had not found this
so. Perhaps because our care of goodness and truth had been
mistaken or inadequate. At any rate, I had watched beauty go
begging for a home and a family. I knew that of the trinity—
goodness, truth and beauty, each an equation for God—beauty is
the most palpable, the most irresistible. I have called it God's
visibility. This explains to me the ever-prevailing diabolism by
which the devil takes such prompt and seductive possession of
physical and human beauty. So perilous a gift is it that God can
scarcely trust us with much at any time in any form. The gross-
ness with which celluloid has exploited the beauty of our young
womanhood sickens me. We wanted to build a home for beauty,
as Gerard Manley Hopkins had said,

> "Give beauty back, beauty, beauty, beauty, back to
> God, beauty's self and beauty's giver."

The cornerstone for the O'Laughlin Auditorium was laid
November 12, 1955, by Bishop Pursley. It bears the inscription
from Chesterton, ART IS THE SIGNATURE OF MAN. Helen Hayes,
First Lady of the American Theater, was the first person to address an audience from the magnificent stage. She quoted to
listeners from coast to coast Portia's great plea, "The quality of
mercy is not strained."

The class of 1956 was the first to graduate from the new auditorium. Honorary degrees were conferred for the first time on the
recipients: His Eminence Francis Cardinal Spellman, our baccalaureate speaker; Walter Kerr, our commencement speaker;
Mother Rose Elizabeth, C.S.C., Jean Charlot, Sister Esther, S.P.,
Helen Hayes, Maria Augusta Trapp, and our veteran trustees:
William Cotter, John O'Laughlin, William Miller, Bernard Voll.

Since that time the O'Laughlin Auditorium has become a home for the NBC Opera Company, with our dear Samuel Chotzinoff and Peter Adler inspiring it, the Ruth Page Chicago Opera Ballet, the South Bend Symphony Orchestra, the South Bend Civic Music Association. Marian Anderson has been one among many great guest artists. Mr. and Mrs. Martin Browne have exemplified the possibilities of the great English Mystery Cycles. Robert Speaight has spent months in successive years directing and producing the best of Shakespeare comedy.

The story is long and, please God, just begun. The chapters on music and art thrill with both promise and accomplishment. The frescoes of Jean Charlot, the designs of Norman Laliberte stand as two cases for many. Our century plant has blossomed.

In defense of a fine arts building, if such is needed, let us remember that the fine arts—poetry, music, the dance—are as old as human history. The writing of books, the liberal arts, developed centuries later. The useful arts are youngest of all. In a capsule, poetry is thousands of years older than soap. I am inclined to rearrange Eric Gill's neat statement to read: "Take care of beauty, and goodness and truth will take care of themselves."

XXIII

Wanting Things Badly Enough

SAINT MARY'S ACADEMY was opened in Bertrand, Michigan, in 1844. In 1855 it was moved six miles south to its present Indiana campus. That campus the academy and the college shared until 1945 when the purchase of the Erskine Estate on Twyckenham Road provided a beautiful home and a dream of a campus for the academy. It released Holy Cross Hall for freshman residence.

With the providential Holy Thursday fire in the old science laboratories and the new science hall, good space on two floors was provided for additional rooms. Summer after summer reconstruction has tried to divide and subdivide possible bedrooms for the increasing enrollments.

The studios vacated by the art department were promptly converted into Queen's Court, the prettiest residence section in Le Mans Hall. All our building for the past twenty years has been for classrooms, and yet we have not enough. None of our building has been for residence. And again, we have not nearly enough.

Our Sister-faculty members live great distances from their classrooms, great distances from their offices. We are wanting a faculty residence hall. Are we wanting it badly enough?

Our student infirmary was among the buildings absorbed in

community reorganization. Our guest facilities shared this process. We are listening to the cry of the home economics department for larger better laboratories. Do we want these badly enough? Who runs this good school? Who takes the blame for things?·

A classroom building, releasing classrooms in Le Mans Hall for residence for one hundred upperclass students presents the least expensive first-aid. It would scarcely care for more than the girls now living in Regina Hall, a building which we rent from our convent, and the forty upperclass students still in Holy Cross Hall. A sister visited us not too long ago to learn something about college administration.

"Do you teach?" she asked.

"No, Sister, I don't," I answered.

"Nothing at all?" in surprise.

"No, I don't," in quasi apology.

"Well, what do you do?"

This is my question exactly now. What do I do? If I want a thing badly enough! How badly can that be? We must have faculty residence, classrooms, home economics laboratories, infirmary.

We have wanted a foreign language laboratory, equipped for listening and recording, available for music and speech as well. It is now installed, thirty-two units, which can be doubled if necessary.

Our library is asking for more carrels, more stack space. A library is the stomach of the school. It must be big and healthy enough to support good intellectual life. It, too, must be fed.

We have wanted a student recreation center, less formal than our parlors, set up for all the amenities of campus life—and for our seven thousand possible guests. From the emerging realities, it would seem that we have wanted this badly enough.

Let us come to the business of college proper, the intellectual life. All of our present faculty we want to remain with us as the

built-in part of our family. We wish that they could be aug-
mented by half as many more equal to them in loyalties and abili-
ties. This would make possible time for research, for writing,
for other creative work. It would provide sabbatical leaves at
proper intervals. For these there is the essential want for funds
to compensate adequately every teacher. These things must come.
We want them badly enough.

I find myself wishing for developed tastes and desires for the
classics, for Greek drama, medieval mystery plays now enjoying
healthy revivals in England and in various centers in our country.
Our sisters and students are learning to evoke music from re-
corders; perhaps the plays will follow the pipers. Then there are
the gracious arts of reading aloud together, of listening to our
great music, of looking at our great art as long and as often as we
would like—and time for these. Time will not be enough. We
shall need forever!

Surely, a goodly company share with me fervent desires for
more students who can spell, read, write; students who can and
will think, who know experimentally that there are no easy
ways and are glad of it. Once in my teacher's life a freshman
came to my office, put her class schedule on my desk and said,
"I am taking these subjects to develop my mind." Who among us
does not hunger and thirst for students to join her in this quest,
who not only "take" subjects but keep them, assimilate them!

I even want students who do not, as Robert Louis Stevenson
has said, "swallow the universe like a pill," girls who know trees
by their first names, who love them better in winter than in
summer and recognize them in their nude beauty. I should like
them to watch for the unfurling of oak leaves in dubious greens,
coral pinks and creams, delicate as the details of some old French
tapestries; beech buds unfolding like small, perfect fans in the
sun. Why shouldn't girls of eighteen mark their spring calendars
by the first bird songs, the first spring wildflowers as well as
by their first orchids? I want them, these girls of ours, to open

their arms, their eyes, their lives wide to the universe, to understand palpably that "Underneath are the everlasting arms." I
want them to be less bewildered with our noisy generation, less
afraid of its loneliness because One who has asked to share it
says, "Be still and know that I am God."

Is this the way to be a teacher? Are these the things to want?

XXIV

The Education of Sister Lucy

For overlong, many of us had struggled with our academic consciences and put the seal of discretion on our lips over the flagrant *status quo* in Catholic education. Even recent indictments of the mediocrity of the Catholic mind scarcely advert to the untrained or inadequately trained sisters who have been teaching generations of parish schoolchildren. The onus of such mental limitations, as are attributed peculiarly to Catholics, has been placed in part on our uncultured immigrant parents.

Permit me this parenthesis: On my father's side, I am the child, on my mother's the grandchild of German immigrants. From the time I was old enough to spend pocket money my father left the cash drawer in his shop at my disposal with the single instruction that I record the amount of money I withdrew. This unique procedure was never questioned or abused. Even now, I honor the memory of my father for the complete and mature and responsible confidence that he placed in me. It was not the attitude of an ignorant or an uncultured parent.

My mother selected and ordered some of the most excellent books in elementary German that I have ever seen. In the north woods in 1890 she knew how and where to buy books. No Book-of-the-Month Club, then nonexistent, could have made choices for her. These and all our books bore this inscription in her clear script: "My books are my friends. Treat them kindly." Now I, with degrees—earned and honorary—and a faculty equally qualified, do not and possibly cannot impress such respect among our students for the textbooks that do so much to fashion their minds. These are bartered for before courses are over. Book sales and exchanges are college business. Last spring, at a meeting of Intellectual and Cultural Affairs, I adverted to this in defense of the uncultured immigrant parent. I was laughed down with the statement that textbooks today deserve no better fate. If so, something is wrong somewhere! Perhaps with the commercialized and lucrative business of making textbooks. But not with our European parents. Professor Gregory Zilboorg, the great, lovable psychologist, came to my rescue:

"I am an immigrant," he said in his big mellow voice. "My mother is illiterate. She can neither read nor write."

End of parenthesis!

To my question, "Why do non-Catholics as a group dislike Catholics?" a very good Quaker friend of mine and a distinguished educator hesitated while I elaborated, "Are they afraid that we will have an American pope or a Catholic president?" Then he answered, "I think that perhaps we do fear your power, but we are jealous of the care that you take of your young people." Here for all time is the case for the Catholic school. With inadequate plants and only partially trained teachers for three hundred years, we have been taking care of our young people. The valor of the achievement is not always patent to us. The non-Catholic sees the sheer courage and conviction in it.

At no time could this be a brief for incomplete teacher preparation. Needs imperative for schools and staff have precipitated young sisters scarcely out of the novitiate into parish schools. For years, a stubborn group of the college section of the National Catholic Educational Association had dreamed of, had asked for a section in the Association for teachers' preparation. Reasons for refusal now seem absurd. Then they were effective, final, and fatal.

At the meeting of the Association in San Francisco in the spring of 1948, I asked for the last time that such a section be authorized and put to work. Approval was overwhelming. The chairmanship of a committee to care for the matter devolved on me. We called a meeting at once of all who were interested. Officers were appointed and plans for our next meeting in Philadelphia begun.

We projected a program in which the training procedures then in operation in six teaching orders were submitted. In addition a possible schedule was formulated by which a young sister beginning her education in a postulancy of one year, continuing through two to three years after her canonical novitiate, could earn her teacher's credentials and degree. The plan was set up for a hypothetical Sister Lucy. It worked beautifully on paper.

Sisters from many communities attended our summer session that year. We chose the nucleus of our program from among them. In the end, papers were assigned to and accepted by Mother M. Eucharista, C.S.J.; Monsignor Clarence E. Elwell; Mother M. Dorothea, O.S.U.; Sister M. Augustine, O.S.F.; Brother Emilian, F.S.C. My own paper presented the problem and our hopes of a solution.

Copies of all the papers were on my desk months before the meeting, excellent, better than I had dreamed, good enough, I knew, for publication. Our new section on Teachers' Education was assigned the smallest committee room, the last hour of the last day of the convention. The room assigned proved absolutely too small. We moved in and out of the cafeteria for the same reason. We settled in the gymnasium with people sitting on the steps and in the aisles. The Education of Sister Lucy proved the big event of the week. The tremendous, spontaneous response to the cause established its importance and its need.

Opening the meeting, I said that the papers to be presented

seemed to me to be eminently worth printing. Through whistling, squealing, temperamental microphones the heroic authors read them. Those present will never forget the hour. At the end the meeting exploded with questions. We were importuned to have the entire texts printed. Within two months a neat brochure, "The Education of Sister Lucy," was off the press at South Bend.

By dexterous choices of nominating committees at our April meeting in Boston in 1950, Monsignor Elwell and Sister Augustine, O.S.F., were elected to office for the coming year. Presently the superior general of the Sisters of the Immaculate Heart at Monroe, Michigan, asked me to come to the mother house to talk over with her council some of the needs, the feasibilities and the professional "musts" of this tentative program. Later, Sister Patrick and her companion came to Saint Mary's to continue planning. Surveying the problems of organization, ways and means, Sister Patrick said, "Sister Emil is just the person to do this." Sister Patrick was right.

When the Institute for Religious held its first great historic meeting at the University of Notre Dame in 1952 I was asked to present the case of completed professional training for religious teachers before they were assigned to their life apostolate of teaching. During that same session Sister Patrick made her memorable plea, "Share the sisters." The facts of sister-shortage, sisters' education, sisters' salaries were emerging. We were coming at this late hour to the use of reason.

Sister Lucy had been admitted to college. I leave her education to those qualified and authorized to educate her, the mothers general, the mothers provincial in the organized Sister-Formation Program.

XXV

The Idea of a University

You will remember that in the strength and confidence of my youth I had incorporated Newman's *The Idea of a University* into a senior English course at Saint Mary's. Most persons know the book for the definition of a gentleman, who most of them never suspect is the perfect social pagan. Newman made clear to me that of all sciences the science of God is the most perfect and that a Christian college should, if consistent, give it the place of pre-eminence in the curriculum, make it the integrating subject, giving sequence, importance and validity to all other subjects. I knew of no liberal arts college organized on this plan. Frank Sheed had said bluntly, and more than once, "There is no place in the United States where a layman can study Theology."

Among prevailing educational affronts and blackouts, this was the worst. In our long and golden age of science we had made no place for, given no thought to the queen of sciences, the science of God. Frank Sheed's statement gave me no peace. Were we to let these flagrancies continue? Even worse, the courses of religion that were offered in our colleges were the dullest and the most poorly taught in the curriculum. We had no graduate schools in which to prepare young teachers of Theology on levels equal to their preparation in profane subjects. Priests qualified to teach Theology were occupied otherwise. Religion was the last and least interesting of all subjects taught by the least prepared and frequently poorest teachers.

In spite of the war, with shattered enrollments, accelerated programs in the men's colleges, the Problems Committee of the National Catholic Educational Association in 1942 decided that the preparation of teachers of religion in college constituted our biggest problem. The task of investigating possibilities and solutions was assigned to me.

No Midwestern college graduate school was prepared to set up the program. The Catholic University answered "No" to our applications to its School of Divinity. Bishop Edwin O'Hara, on our campus for a day, suggested Saint Mary's as a proper place. I demurred at the seeming presumption of the thought.

"The place is ideal," the Bishop suggested, "living conditions excellent, beautiful spiritual resources, a fine library. May the Executive Director of the Confraternity of Christian Doctrine authorize the opening of a School of Sacred Theology at Saint Mary's?"

Overwhelmed, and authorized by his rhetorical question, I thanked him and began a new chapter in Catholic education. Frank Sheed would finally be answered.

At the next meeting of the College Section of the NCEA I reported my failure to get help from our graduate schools. Everyone understood the reasons: war, G.I.'s, acceleration. We were at a dead end. Had anyone any ideas? No one broke the impasse. Then, with that strange impulse outside my will, I stood up and said:

"I do not know how we will do it, but this summer we will offer at Saint Mary's a six-weeks' graduate program in Theology, without tuition and without credit. I regret that we shall have to make a nominal charge for maintenance. We will send you details in a fortnight."

Everyone thought the gesture promising and thanked me. Then we went home.

Father Gerald Ellard, S.J., was in the midst of a triduum for the students of Saint Mary's when I arrived. I told him my story and asked his help.

"I am with Father Lord's Circus this summer and have only one free week," he said to me.

"All right, come that week and teach double time," I clinched the possibility.

"Why don't you ask Father Gruenthaner?" he said. "He will be free and would like to come, I believe." This proved true.

Monsignor William Newton had one week free. Their times clicked miraculously. We had three teachers, doing double time, in succession, for six weeks.

Eighteen sisters registered in June, 1943. Monsignor Newton initiated the school. Father Ellard followed. The experience was pentecostal. Father Michael Gruenthaner, S.J., arrived for the final month. He taught from a Hebrew text; he dramatized the Pentateuch. He knew every sister by name. He read all the funnies. He went to all the movies. Physically, he resembled Chesterton. In every way, he was the big person on the faculty.

At the end of two weeks I tried to talk to him about plans for the next year. He evaded me. At the end of the third week he was equally elusive. Finally, I corralled him in that old curiosity shop, my inner office.

"Father," I said, "our need for graduate work in Scripture and Theology is obvious. What can we do?"

"You haven't the curriculum," he said gruffly.

"I know," I answered helplessly, "and I don't know how to make one; but you do and I think that you should help me."

"You have no graduate library," his second objection.

"That is true, and until now we haven't needed one. But with a thousand dollars a year don't you think that you could buy a few books?" I countered.

"You haven't got a faculty," as if to overwhelm me.

"Father," I said, "if the Church has no one to teach us our religion, then I think that the Church has failed."

At this time I did not know that his first three answers were never his real ones. He peered at my indignant face from under his bushy eyebrows like a Hebrew prophet.

"I have said everything that I can to discourage you," he said gently. "Now I think that I will try to help you."

So the School of Sacred Theology came into being: curriculum, library, faculty, chancellor.

To honor it, to honor the centenary of our community and our collegiate foundation, Bishop O'Hara and the Episcopal Committee of the Confraternity of Christian Doctrine, under whose auspices the new translation of the New Testament was authorized, held their three-day conferences at Saint Mary's during the summers of 1943 and 1944.

With Father Gruenthaner, he was instrumental in obtaining the approval of the Holy Father, through the ministration of His Eminence Cardinal Pizzardo.

The school, now fifteen years old, has initiated graduate study of Sacred Theology and Scripture far beyond the United States. From the beginning, students from Europe and India have enrolled. Because of it, I believe, I was invited to membership on the Executive Committee for Women Religious of the United States of America, the only member not a superior general.

This committee met for the first time at the University of Notre Dame in 1952. During this first Institute for Religious, the secretaries of The Most Reverend Arcadio Larraone, and Father Paul Philippe, O.P., himself, spent hours in discussing our program, assembling literature and textbooks for use in Rome. They were incorporated, I believe, in the program of Regina Mundi, the graduate school of Theology for sisters, opened in 1953 in Rome.

For fifteen years our great teaching communities of men:

Holy Cross, Jesuits, Precious Blood have filled our need for teachers with their best. Congruously, but also generously, the provincials of the Dominican Fathers have staffed our graduate and undergraduate schools with teachers who make Theology and Scripture the best courses in the curricula. We can never replace or repay them.

Father Leo Arnoult, O.P., Sister Augustella, and Ann Condit are engaged in a monumental work of selecting, collecting and translating writings of the Fathers on Sacramental Grace. Father Mark Egan, now our chancellor, with his zealous staff collects and circulates weekly among the faculty current pronouncements from the Holy Father on subjects relating to their departments or their interests. They entitle their project, significantly, "The Living Voice of Christ."

We are here, Cardinal Newman, at Saint Mary's. Theology is the queen of sciences and the integrating core of the entire academic life of the college. Once Saint Thomas might have had to prove that women have souls. Now he can regard happily their Thomistic minds and the home in which they honor his *Summa*.

XXVI

A Thousand Girls and
Seven Thousand Boys

AT THE end of my year in Europe I asked Sister Verda Clare, "What have you missed most from home this year?" I don't remember her answer, but mine was, "Not the coffee and not the plumbing. What I have missed most is the American girl." I believe that I would have the same answer today. All but six of these my first seventy years have been spent in school, more than fifty in boarding school, living with, breaking bread with American girls, not by the dozen but the hundreds and thousands. Since I have traded myself in to God for all potential daughters, He has given me this family of girls to live with and for, to love.

Let me name just a sampling: the little brown-eyed girl who used to dress up in her mother's wedding dress to write to me and who has never failed over forty years to send a Christmas candle; the pink-and-white girl who used to pick up spots of moonlight on the stair landings going up to bed; the enigmatic girl for whom the law of contradiction did not exist and whom, for all that, I persisted in believing in. The mountain hikers, the wildflower lovers, the first robin girls know who they are. And so does the girl who never handed in her compositions, the one who always did, the girl who spelled *and* with two *d*'s; the two true loves who named their daughters "Madeleva," both eventually going through Saint Mary's as "Junior." Where is the friend who always brought a rose back from town, the one with whom I walked under an umbrella in the snow? Where are you, my dear, who shattered my world one day at lunch by asking innocently, "Sister, did you ever teach?"

And, Anne, do you remember your coming to my office, overwhelmed by a sense of duty, to ask,

"Sister, I wonder if you know how dissatisfied the girls are with Saint Mary's."

"Well, Anne," I answered you, "perhaps I don't. But do the girls know how dissatisfied I am with Saint Mary's? No one is half so dissatisfied as I."

"You," you exclaimed incredulously.

Then I explained:

"Suppose that at eighteen you were all perfectly satisfied: what would you have to work for, to try for? Suppose that we were filled with complacency about school, what petrified big and little prigs we would be? Eighteen is the time at which to be dissatisfied, to be reaching out, to be looking up."

Sometimes, when asked how many students we have I answer facetiously:

"Over a thousand girls and seven thousand boys."

In many ways, the second half of my count is untrue. Many Notre Dame men are now married. Many more never come over to Saint Mary's campus. Their reasons are good and usually rest on common sense. But the presence of seven thousand college men on our horizon contributes subtly and, I am sure, very constructively to our world. We know it to be the ideal situation for social life, intercollegiate dramatics, music, debate.

I want to submit these few campus nephew friendships of my own. Twenty years ago a young law student from San Francisco came into my office with Sister Marie Rosaire. He was interested in printing and in Christian art. "Harry, why don't you make some bookmarks, vertical, but good texts, good type, paper, design?" I asked. Harry acted on the suggestion. The designs were executed in our art studios. Harry did the printing in his small shop in South Bend. This was the beginning of the Berliner McGinnis printing business now located in Nevada City, California, and an authentic exponent of Christian art.

One day during the war, four servicemen, all non-Catholic, came over from Notre Dame to call. They had been students at Saint John's College, Annapolis. President Stringfellow Barr and Dean Scott Buchanan, both my good friends, had told them to come over for a visit. After a bit of small talk, I suggested that we discuss something serious, something up to the level of Saint John's; eschatology, for instance. The result of our talk on the four last things—death, judgment, hell, heaven—was more visits, fine stimulating discussion, and a gift from one of them of T. S. Eliot's *Four Quartets*. Presently the boys left for overseas. One of them wrote, "Imagine my delight in picking up in a London bookshop the other day a beautiful edition of Saint Thomas' *Treatise on the Angels*. This was a not unhappy sequel to our talk on the four last things."

A Mother's Day brought me another quartet of Notre Dame boys. They wanted copies of my verse for gifts to their mothers. After providing these, I said,

"I have a gift for each of you from your Mother also." I gave each a copy of Saint Louis-Marie Grignion de Montfort's *True Devotion to the Blessed Virgin*.

More than a year later, I was called to the Great Hall. A handsome, Spanish-looking boy smiled at me.

"You don't remember me," he said.

I didn't.

"You gave us some books more than a year ago and we didn't pay you for them," he volunteered.

"I didn't expect you to. We charged that to administration," I explained.

"Have you any more of those books?" he asked, putting twenty dollars in my hand.

"You must have managed your allowance well to save all this," I commented.

"I wait on table," he said.

Until his graduation we negotiated with copies of Saint Louis de Montfort's classic, the distribution of which he made an apostolate among the students. After a brilliant graduate career in France, he retraced the journeys of Saint Paul and of Saint Thomas as far as Goa in India before returning to America to teach philosophy in one of our excellent Eastern colleges. This is a long Mother's Day story.

One other campus nephew you must meet. He came over at the end of freshman year to tell me that he was not returning to Notre Dame, that he was going to the University of Chicago to get into the Great Books course. He spoke with some satisfaction of the Great Books he had read: Plato, Aristotle, Saint Thomas.

"Have you read the greatest book, Michael? Have you read the Bible?" I asked.

"No," he stuttered.

"Have you a Bible?"

Again he stuttered, "No."

"Michael, don't come over again until you have got yourself a Bible and have begun reading it!"

This was our goodbye for the summer.

He wrote during the vacation, reporting on having read the Bible, not once but twice; and returned to Notre Dame to finish in liberal arts.

With his military service fulfilled in Europe, his Doctorate in philosophy from a graduate school in France, he is now a Dominican Scholastic in the Middle West.

Four are a small but a good fraction of our seven thousand

boys. I seem to have said overmuch for them in proportion to my girls. For these latter are mine by that divine CPA system by which God pays me back a hundredfold of His promise always and in all ways. For His reasons, which are mine and more, I love them, collectively and individually, every *A, B, C, D* and *E* girl of them. The *E's* particularly. To the confusion of screening boards, what a surprising number of these dear young geese have grown into impressive, efficient swans! Many of them are now well over thirty, over forty. Daughters of not a few are Saint Mary's graduates, Saint Mary's mothers. What did I teach them? I have for answer perhaps the most astounding revelation of my life.

Gladys had come back to school to visit. We had not seen each other for years. Falling into an old-fashioned pattern, we walked on the river bank. Gladys had been a slow student, not always able to separate fact from fancy.

"Sister," she said with conviction, "there is one thing that you taught us that I shall never forget."

I purred with satisfaction. She reasserted her statement, past all possibilities of doubt. She agreed with me, she said, absolutely.

"What is this impressive truth, Gladys," I asked, "that I taught you that you will never forget?"

"Sister," she replied, "you taught us that there is no hell!"

Gladys has been with God now for these many years. He has blessed her with a Jesuit son and has, I hope, vindicated me.

For the past twenty-five years the invisible but palpable screen of administration has obscured me from our students much more than them from me. Personal acquaintance with a thousand is impossible. The amenities of meals with seniors, conferences with student officers always leave us better friends than they found us. In convocations I try to convince all Saint Mary's girls that they will never be more intelligent than they are in college. They will add to their stature by putting over the denominators of their intelligence the numerators of experience. This will change

throughout their entire lives. I ask them to believe the boy
friends who tell them that they are beautiful. Only the boys cannot know how beautiful they are or why. Being God's daughters
they must resemble Him. Because He is beauty, they must be
beautiful. This is not a cosmetic concession. It is a family duty.
Sometimes at convocations I suggest that we take off our bodies
and sit in our souls. The experience, however vicarious, has
values.

Thinking of James Bridie's *Tobias and the Angel,* we put
the boy friends in competition with their guardian angels. Crew
cuts become less irresistible when seen in angelic light. By the
same token, their own transcendence may suffer, set beside that
of their own angels. Even so, watching them through the fugitive
loveliness of their final teens, I wish that their parents could
know their daughters as I do. Physical maternity and paternity
are divine impelling forces of life. In her intellectual maternity,
the religious teacher gives to her children the unique supernatural integrity of virginal love. Often, watching generations
of girls living their four-year span of college life, I have quoted
to myself Christopher Fry's:

> "O, God, the fabulous wings unused
> Folded in the heart"

following it with this other, describing superlatively Saint Mary's
part in their upbringing:

> "Lives make and unmake themselves in her neighborhood
> As nowhere else."

XXVII

Educating Our Daughters as Women

At this spring's meeting of our board of lay trustees one report was submitted that is basic to our consideration, that of the president of the college. This report made particular mention of the major and minor fields in which students were qualifying, or had already qualified, particularly in medical technology, in the nursing arts, in teaching. Attention focused rather sharply on specializations. We took a look at the advisability of training mathematicians for certain areas of engineering, of artists and photographers for commercial advertising.

The real objective of the students' education began to be pretty tangential. One blue-ribbon trustee asked the quietly innocent question, "Does anyone think of educating a woman as a woman?"

We were all pulled back sharply into place. We found ourselves facing the basic double problem in education which I now submit to you. Should college educate a woman as a woman? If so, how? These are good questions. They suggest this third equally important one: Do all types of colleges educate our daughters equally well in their proper vocation of being women?

Running the gantlet of semantics, we may say that we always educate a woman as a woman. The quantity and quality of her womanhood depend very much, first upon herself, then upon the school that she attends, the school that is her Alma Mater. She will probably resemble her intellectual mother. I think that our trustee had in mind a quintessence of womanliness as a quality to be preserved, if not indeed to be developed in the education of our daughters. We, too, believe in the quintessence of womanliness as the very flower and fruit of the education of women.

These daughters of ours have had two choices in the kind of college training they wished: coeducation or education in the private college for women. They have chosen the latter. They have elected to be educated as women with an existential major and minor in womanhood. Their academic choices become effective in this environment, in this their essential existence. Their entire life, their worlds, their uncounted futures have already received certain determinations, certain directions by this momentous choice.

They might have gone to coeducational schools. Why not? Coeducational universities and colleges educate young women in exactly the same way as they educate men. In fact all our coeducational schools on the college level, until within the past decade perhaps, began as schools for men. Women were admitted first cautiously and by exception. Once matriculated, they proved, by and large, their ability to be educated as men or in curricula set up for men. Departments in home economics and nursing were gradually provided specifically for them. Today women constitute a large per cent of the enrollment in coeducational schools. Tens of thousands of our American girls are in college with hundreds of thousands of our American boys, and love it. They emerge as educated women, but not quite the same type of women they might have been if they had been educated as women.

These are merely statements of fact. They are neither a measure of the value of coeducation to our daughters, nor of our daughters to coeducation. No one expects the winner of a Vogue contest to run even a handicap with a fifth horseman of the historic Rockne four. No one weighs Miss America in the same balance as a varsity basketeer. But the value of girls on the coeducational campus is even greater, let me dare to say, more pervasive, more subtle, if you do not mind the overworked word. It has something to do with ties, with crew cuts, even with the gentle arts of courtesy. Recently our local newspaper published the picture of a student carrying his girl friend's books. This was front-page news. Upon a time our best American university (according to the Chicago *Tribune*) reported that the registration of two pretty young women in the graduate school had effected a palpable return to the fine arts and courtesies of living among these superlative men students.

Girls do not go to coeducational schools for these reasons, but they do affect coeducation in these ways. Reciprocally, their coeducational colleges affect them. A girl, educated with and as boys are educated, will be a different woman from the girl educated as girls are and with them.

This does not imply that they are or should be educated exclusively by women. The better the college for women, the healthier ballast of scholarly men it will invite to its faculty. The mind of a growing girl realizes its capacities more perfectly under the tutelage of both scholarly men and scholarly women. This is equally true for boys. Men are quick and proud to recognize this.

But as boys, they do not clamor to go to colleges for women; they do not stampede our private schools and insist on being educated as girls are educated. We women have reversed the story of the Sabine women; we have put ourselves in a somewhat unintellectual position in our very endeavor to prove our intellectual equality with men.

For more than a century and a quarter our girls have had excellent colleges for women from which to choose. They select this type of school because they want this experience of the intellectual life as and with young women. Most of them do not change their minds on this score during their four undergraduate years. Since 1898 Saint Mary's College has been granting Bachelors' degrees to these daughters of hers.

Just how does she educate young women as women? She recognizes the great fields of knowledge, the sciences, the liberal arts, the fine arts. Since Theology is the queen of the sciences she makes it the core, the central and integrating subject in the curriculum. The student's entire experience becomes significant in terms of its relation to God. The student herself grows in the knowledge of her own supernatural stature in consequence, and of the supernatural world itself in which we all live and move. Her womanhood is measured by, and uplifted to the womanhood of Mary. This in itself educates her as a woman.

Around the science of Theology, the profane sciences range themselves in orders and potencies which atomic energies and electronics merely shadow. Women can move among these as freely as men, with the authentic freedom of truth. Such fields as cancer research, the care of premature babies are being successfully investigated by teachers and students in Catholic colleges for women. They are living in their Father's house, working with His tools, playing at times perhaps with the fascinating toys He has provided for them. This is far from fancy. The greatest scientists know it to be a divine fact.

The liberal arts are most liberal, most liberating when they rest on complete rather than on partial truth. Here the Catholic college is the authentic exponent for the first sixteen centuries of Christian arts and sciences. One may say the same of the fine arts.

Our presentation seems to move to the Catholic versus the non-Catholic school irrespective of coeducation. This would be true if it were not equally true that girls study, learn, and respond to teaching differently from the way boys do, and differently in classes with boys from in groups of girls only. Whatever the reasons for the delicate psychology governing these facts, they are facts. Girls achieve a type of womanhood when educated with girls which differs from the results of coeducation. We believe that this difference is a more refined, a more perfect womanhood, the quintessential womanliness which our blue-ribbon trustee had in mind.

Perfection is not achieved without costs. The women's colleges in the United States are monuments to the enterprise, the sacrifice, the fortitude of women. They are the most expensive to maintain, the last to benefit by philanthropy. Present educational crises are being met by colossal gifts from corporations, foundations, individuals.

At a recent meeting of the American Council on Education, the question was asked, "Where in the order of these gifts do colleges for women stand?" This is the answer which was given, not without embarrassment: "Gifts for education go, first, to schools with big names; second, to big schools; third, to co-educational schools; fourth, to women's colleges." We might add, last of all to Catholic women's colleges. Considering that half the parents of the world, all the mothers, the wives, the daughters, and the sisters are women this does not reflect gloriously to the generosity, the chivalry, the gratitude, or even the justice of the manhood of our country.

Yet, up and down our nation, these schools for our daughters are strongholds of the sciences, the liberal arts, the fine arts. As Pitirim Sorokin said in his address on "The Fine Arts in the College Curriculum" at a meeting of the Association of American Colleges last January: "Like the early medieval monasteries [they] are still the main centers of the history . . . and techniques of art with all of the *what, how* and *why* involved." Handfuls of sisters in our teaching communities of women, with or without money, are making this possible. They believe in educating our daughters as women. Years ago, Coventry Patmore wrote in a prelude to *The Angel in the House:*

"Ah, wasteful woman, she who may
    On her sweet self set her own price,
Knowing man cannot choose but pay,
    How has she cheapen'd paradise;
How given for nought her priceless gift,
    How spoil'd the bread and spill'd the wine,
Which, spent with due, respective thrift,
    Had made brutes men, and men divine."

The Sisters of the Holy Cross believe this. Saint Mary's College is their act of faith.

XXVIII

Dear Parents

For a quarter of a century you and I have been working together on the biggest, best business in the world, the business of education. That, for all of us, focused on your daughters. Don't you think that this is a good time and a good place for us to compare notes? I think that we will all love the experience. For purposes of narrative, let us take our daughters who are graduating this year.

Sixteen years ago you took your six-year-old daughters to school, to the first grade for the first time. I dare say that your memories of those little girls on that first day are among the most vivid of your lives.

For eight years you read and signed report cards and proudly chronicled the academic events of promotion. Came a day when this elementary intellectual progress reached its appointed climax. These daughters were graduated from the eighth grade. You have not forgotten the succession of flutters in which matter prevailed over mind and the eighth-grade graduation dresses competed in importance with the little girls who were in them.

September brought the sequel. On the Tuesday morning following Labor day, a bevy of very, very young ladies, a bit shy, a bit assured, entered high school. Your own educational pace

quickened. Your own vocabularies jolted themselves into the un-
canny canniness of high school language. Your own little girls
were growing up almost too fast for you. Between the curricular
and the extracurricular causes that educated, where was the pause
that refreshed! With or without it, you hurried on through high
school with these daughters, at typical American tempo. How well
you share with them, but for different reasons, the memories of
the first date, the first formal, perhaps the first orchid. There were,
too, the school paper, the class ring, the glee club, the class play
and—the team.

The wonder of Advent, the mystery of Christmas, the prophetic
realities of Lent and Easter unfolded as your daughters shared
their deeper, holier high school experiences with you.

For four years you went to high school again. You relearned
their lessons with these keen, bright girls who matched your
minds but not your hearts, not your maturity.

Again you are swept out of the routine of class and homework
into the climactic week of high school graduation. Somewhere
in the limitless bright procession of flowers, cameras, cars, academic regalia, speeches, diplomas one gathers that here again an
epoch in the intellectual life of your daughters has come to its
end.

Sometime during the past four years you or they or all of you
from many wheres in the United States and out of it had written
to Saint Mary's College, Notre Dame, Indiana, for bulletins and
other information, for application blanks and room reservations.
By the beautiful mystery of the providence of God, lines of interest, attraction, decision all converged on this single place, this now
beloved Alma Mater. It became your school long before you
arrived with the first cargo of college impedimenta. You were all
going to college.

When you arrived, Sisters of the Holy Cross welcomed you,
lay faculty received you, big sisters identified themselves to their
brand new little sisters. Elevators served you and sisters on the

floors helped to set up the household gods in the daughters' rooms. And in that blessed oasis at the north end of the first floor of Holy Cross Hall you came to rest and the pause that refreshes— alumnae hospitality unlimited.

These daughters from out of the everywhere, with you their parents, matriculated as college freshmen and entered the field of undergraduate study. The sequel you may know perhaps more intimately than I do: the five days of work each week, with the two days of play that kept your Jills from being dull girls.

Who among the students does not recall every incident in that confused and apocalyptic first week, from the testing programs to the W.R.A. Mixer? Finally first things emerged: class cards, textbooks, teachers. In three miraculous days your daughters with that almost intuitive competence of youth had become, externally at least, self-reliant, up-and-coming freshmen, ready for the intellectual life ahead.

The surf and spray of first week activities had drawn back, leaving them and you in the deep sea of the Trivium. All of you have had your desperate struggle swimming it, sailing it, or walking on its difficult waters. But in spite of real or imagined dangers, not one of you drowned.

Freshman year was a year of firsts: the first Sunday, the first home game, the first victory dance, the first retreat, the first Christmas party, the freshman formal, the first May procession at Saint Mary's.

Presently you found your daughters back at school, sophomores, assured, experienced, wisely efficient. They have had and can never forget the feeling of returning to school, as to home, of running up to their old rooms with their new occupants, of finding their own in Le Mans Hall. There was a whole summer to live over with friends in the brief day before classes began.

Then with an interruption scarcely more palpable than the ordinary weekend, school was in full session and so were you. What did our synchronized program of adult and sophomore education offer us this year: psychology, English, some intimations of what your majors were to be in your choices of sciences and mathematics.

Almost at once the students were involved in the Play Tournament, the Christmas play, Winter Carnival, Variety Show. What was the theme of the Cotillion, and what formals did they wear? The memories were as dear as the questions were vital. On Memorial Day the class presented a large American flag to the school. Six of your daughters carried it up to the altar in the chapel of the Holy Ghost to be blessed. Later they raised and saluted it, then lowered it to half-mast as they marched to the cemetery of Our Lady of Peace. There they visited the graves of the Sisters of the Holy Cross who had served our country as nurses in wartime.

Freshman year was a time of planting, sophomore year a time of growth, junior year was the flowertime of all their college days. Theirs was the Christmas party, the junior prom; theirs with seniors the yearbook, and cap and gown night. Theirs were the upper-class privileges, more desired at times than even a *magna cum laude.* Better than these were the growing maturity of judgment with which they began to weigh and to determine values, the sense of responsibility with which they approached the question of their vocations, God's will for them and their lives. Almost from their first week as freshmen they had found classes in Theology absorbing. Now some of them wanted to major in this queen of sciences, or at least to take as many electives as possible in it. Fathers, mothers, families, friends, all met on this the highest, holiest level of their lives.

In September the students returned to Saint Mary's for the final fruit-gathering year of this academic planting and sowing. There was poignancy, even then, as they greeted one another and began doing for the last time the things grown dear by three years of repetition and habit. The Mass of the Holy Spirit for the opening of school had never been so solemn as this year when they marched to chapel for the first time in senior cap and gown.

The Christmas play, always dramatically beautiful and spiritually exalting, had never moved them more deeply. As guests at the perfect Christmas party, they realized a place of honor and such hospitality as only Saint Mary's can accord to her senior daughters. Later in the evening, until almost midnight in fact, gathered around the glory of the lighted Christmas tree and the blazing hearth fire, through that last hour of story and song and silence they knew deeply the love of Saint Mary's for her children, and of the child's love in the heart of each of them for this mother.

Dear parents, do you recognize the story; do you remember it? What have we forgotten? Long-distance calls, weekends at home, happy birthdays, the family rosary, the boy friends, your growing pride and joy in these growing girls who can share with you solid judgments on social and economic issues of the day, important allocutions of our Holy Father, gifts of art, music, speech; daughters who can return to you in wardrobes of their own construction and serve you dinners of their own cooking. You had sent them to college to learn to think for themselves, to form right judgments in the right ways, to live graciously with others, to prepare themselves, each one, for the great business of being a good woman. We hope that you are satisfied that their fulfillment has matched your desire.

Forgotten now is all the anguish of comprehensives, for joy that all these B.A.'s and B.S.'s are born into the world. Not to be forgotten is the final formal senior ball, the final Solemn Mass and dedication to Our Lady and her Seat of Wisdom. Each one of these held in itself an essential dedication of all your futures, a life with Mary in God.

For four years they have lived this life in the daily Mass, sung or spoken in dialogue with the celebrant, their active lay apostolate of teaching, social service, prayer, personal holiness. Students and parents have shared these years of college life and study. Together you can take back to a wider world this life of liturgical thinking and acting, this life of work and worship. Supposing you knew that your neighbor's home stood over the richest oil deposit in the world. Would you tell him, or would you let him live and die in ignorance of this great wealth? The fact is that millions of persons are living in potential possession of faith, the richest treasure in the world. You know the truth of this faith. Won't you tell your neighbors of it? Think of the men who have died for us for lesser goods. Tell your neighbors of the oil wells of truth under their house of life.

More than half of the people in the world are spiritual orphans. They do not know where they came from or where they are going. They do not know that God is their Father. They do not even know of His existence. You do. Would you keep the knowledge of their human father from orphans? Will you let an orphan-world live and die without even knowing this Father who has blessed you so much beyond His gifts to them? Will you not reclaim at least some of your spiritual brothers and sisters in the name of God, our Father?

A Catholic education is, as you know, an investment in eternity. Your new car will be old in a year. Presently it will have to be replaced. The child you educate in a Christian school is immortal. This education will never have to be replaced. It will last forever, and by that I mean *forever*. The school that you help to educate that child is in business with God for Him. The Catholic college is God's idea of education. He has let you share it. You have just completed vicariously a four-year college program with and for your daughters. Do you believe in it?

The American Council on Education published several years ago a book entitled *The Function of the Public Schools in Dealing with Religion*. To quote from the late Dr. George F. Zook, then president of the Council:

> "There is almost universal complaint that education has become too much a matter of learning facts and that there is altogether too little emphasis upon values and objectives.

The schools and churches are therefore confronted with a common problem, but, because of the prevailing separation of church and state in this country, there is relatively little cooperation between religious organizations and the public schools. How to bring about a reconsideration of the relation of religion to education was the central theme of the conference."

The Catholic college exists for the purpose of defining and fulfilling the function of education in the matter of religion. The place of religion is the basic, the first place. So rooted, all other education becomes truly significant, even sanctified. All knowledge then reflects God's omniscience. The lowliest matter displays the wonder of His creative art. Only when we know matter as God's creation do we truly know it, can we love and use it intelligently. Only when we know the world as God's world and the place of His love can we be happily at home in it, can we be literally and holily secular.

Our journey into the past ends with a journey into the future. We know that it is precarious. We foresee that it will be hard. We tease ourselves with questions about peace, about security, forgetting that such security as many seek is mortal's chiefest enemy. You, parents, have sought at Saint Mary's and have received precepts of peace, the tranquillity of ordered thinking, the disciplined training of an educated mind, a will sacramentally fortified, a life directed by and to God. It has been said that we are secure only when we can stand everything that can happen to us. On these terms I believe that you are secure. On these terms I ask you to take the peace of God, the security of God, as you know them, to your world.

XXIX

Lucy Rehearses Her Funeral

LUCY as you know is my mother. We often called her by her
Christian name by way of endearment. She had no other given
name. She needed none. The bright clarity of this unambiguous
dissyllable was a lifetime mission to her and light to us. She always
dared to be her name.

Lucy died of being ninety-four years old. The last two weeks of
her life she spent in Saint Mary's Hospital, Duluth, Minnesota,
of no other illness than this.

She was sitting up in bed when I arrived in her room from an
overnight train trip. A white bed jacket cuddled around her
shoulders. Her cheeks pink with excitement, her snowy hair
caught back in soft waves by a narrow ribbon tied in a bow at
the top of her head, her eager smiling eyes gave her the look of
a little girl ninety-four years young. A pink carnation tucked
in her hair ribbon added a dear touch of coquetry.

I had been summoned the day before to what the doctors
thought might be the flickering out of the bright keen candle of
my mother's life. We greeted each other with broken bits of
happy laughter, question, answer.

"Mother was good to let you come," she said, referring to
the religious superior of my community.

"We all know that you are the only mother that matters now," I assured her. "All the sisters send you their love and prayers. You know that you and father are everybody's sweethearts at the convent."

"Your father and the boys will be here later. We spend as much time as we can together," she said, adding, "Do you think that God is going to take me?"

"That is His secret, Mother," I answered. "No one would blame Him. You look and are so dear and good. It will be a tremendous experience for our little Lucy and one we want to share as intimately as we can with you."

Then most abruptly, "What shall I say when I see God?" she asked. One can hardly be prepared for so big a question. Trying to collect both my scattered wits and wisdom,

"Mother, say 'Glory be to the Father and to the Son and to the Holy Ghost,'" I answered.

"Yes," came her quick rejoinder, "and I'll say, 'God, be merciful to me, a sinner.' For what do I need so much as His mercy, and if I have that what else do I need?" I agreed that her theology more than covered her needs and God's judgment.

We visited quietly during the day. Afternoon brought my father and two brothers. We planned that I should remain with mother until eleven when the night nurse came on. As I left her, shortly before midnight, our little sick-abed lady asked:

"Do you think God will come for me tonight?"

"No, Mother, I don't," I assured her.

"Why not?" she persisted with a shade of disappointment in her voice.

"You seem very well and strong to me," I answered.

"Yes," she said, quite as a matter of fact, "a person who can drink a bowl of soup and a cup of tea for supper isn't so badly off, is she? But if I need you, you will come, won't you?"

I promised her that I should be there at a moment's call as I kissed her good night and made a small sign of the Cross on her forehead.

By eight-thirty next morning I was back at her bedside, to find her neat and sweet and very much alive.

"You see, God doesn't want me yet," she laughed. Then continued, "What are you going to do with me after I die?"

"We will bury you, Mother," I said. "How would you like to be buried?" I guessed that our little dictator wanted to arrange all the details of her own burial.

"Put my black and white dress on me, unless there is another that you like better," she conceded, "and put new stockings on me. Don't let the undertakers doll me up. You know I always liked simple things. Mrs. Jacobson never had her hair curled until she was dead. Don't let them doll me up!"

I assured her that we would protect her from mortuary beauticians.

"Have you thought of your pallbearers?" I asked, knowing that she wanted this cue.

"Oh! yes. There are the nephews—four of them, the two Jameses, Frederic, John. Then ask Stephen Algeo and Bill Cavanaugh, if he is out of service. Sometimes"—she paused as the pageant unfolded before her, "sometimes there are honorary pallbearers. I would like Mollie and Marie, Kate and Mrs. Mirwald. I can see it all now! And be sure to put new stockings on me." She smiled contentedly as she watched in admiration the cortege of her own funeral move down the hushed main street of Cumberland, the small Wisconsin town where eventually she would be buried.

Presently I began rearranging books and flowers on the dresser. From her bed mother undertook to correct my housekeeping.

"Mother," I laughed, "you will always be a better housekeeper than I am. I may perhaps write better books but not keep a better home."

"Yes," she caught me up, "and if I had had your chance I

could do much better than you do!" This valiant little woman never gave any of us an inch on which to stand.

That afternoon father and my two brothers came. During our visit, in a spell of physical weakness, mother asked,

"Do you think that I am dying?"

"No," we said, "but would you like to have us say some prayers?"

"Yes," she answered, and responded to all of them as well as any of us. Then she turned to my father.

"Did you hear what Sister said?" she asked.

"Yes, Lucy, I did."

"Will you keep these things always in mind?"

"I surely will."

"And will you always be firm in your faith?"

"I certainly will."

"I used to hope," she continued to my father, "that you might die first. I thought that perhaps I could help you. But as long as God has decided differently this way is best."

The next afternoon the five of us were together again and alone. Said mother,

"Do you think that I have failed in my duties to you as a wife and a mother?" Abashed, we answered,

"Surely not; we have often failed you, but you have never failed us."

"I have been severe with you at times," she said, "but it was because I loved you so much that I did not want you to do anything that might separate you from God. I think that I have always loved God, even before I knew how to love Him." Before this theology, this intuitive knowledge, this supernatural charity we had nothing to say. We had been taken beyond the areas or the needs of speech.

Days were passing. Our dear patient seemed in no immediate danger. The years had taught us something of her amazing recuperative powers. So I said cautiously,

"Mother, don't you think it time that I get back to my work?"

"You have permission to be here," she protested.

"Yes, and I will stay if you think that I should. The boys have their work that they must attend to, and I have mine," I answered even more cautiously. She looked knowingly at the nurse.

"It is too bad that we didn't raise our children to be maids," she laughed, then quoted:

> "Duty points with outstretched fingers;
> Straight the path, austere and high.
> Woe betide the soul that lingers.
> Onward, upward is the cry!"

"You see, I have a lecture engagement in Saint Louis within the week. If I am to keep it I shall have to leave tomorrow. But if you wish, I can wire and cancel my appointment," I explained.

Came the quick challenge, "How much do you receive for these lectures?"

I named a very generous honorarium.

"Will that help you to save your soul?"—a second challenge.

"Yes, Mother," I said, stung to defense, "I think it will. I never speak without trying to do some good."

"Yes," she answered, "I believe you."

The next evening we said our last goodbye. Still sitting up in bed as I had found her a week before, pink-cheeked, eyes shining with unshed tears, smiling she sent me on my way.

" 'Duty points,' " she quoted,

" 'Onward, upward is the cry!' "

Four days later, a long-distance telephone message came. The brave bright candle of the life that was Lucy had burned out. Mother had answered her own momentous question,

"What shall I say when I see God?"

Mother's funeral, for which she had so happily instructed us, took place quite as she had wished, on a bright day in early May.

My father went back with my brothers to Duluth where he lived for the next five years in the lovely McCabe Home, under the care of the good Benedictine Sisters. For years the thought of possible separation after death had troubled him. It acted, I think, as the preventing grace for his becoming a Catholic some years before. Here, with a chapel just across from his room, he could go to Mass daily, say his rosary, and keep his promise to Lucy: always to be strong in his faith.

He loved growing old and hoped that he would live to be a hundred. We made much of his birthday after mother's death. September 10 was the day. With her picture enthroned on the table, the four of us had the annual party with candles, cake and presents. On the afternoon of the last of these parties he and I had been walking in the orchard and garden for a pleasant hour. The ripening fruit, the laden branches pleased him. Again and again he would point out lovely colorings or beautiful groupings of crab apples. A bit tired, we sat quietly in the sun, neither of us saying anything. Then he asked me, half-puzzled, half-incredulous, "Where have you been, Lucy, all this time?" No question has ever told me so much. That instant of being his possible Lucy remains in my memory dear beyond a lifetime of being his actual daughter. In a moment, the illusion had passed. He did not try to explain.

Once more before God came for him I saw him. As I came into the room, the nurse said, "Mr. Wolff, your daughter, Sister Madeleva, is here to visit you. You remember her, don't you?" He took my busy hands in his quiet ones, looked earnestly into my face and said, "You must be she." He would make no second mistake. I could not be Lucy again.

His death was a sleep and an awakening. We put him beside her on another May morning, six years after her funeral. A simple granite stone, two markers and a blue spruce guard their graves.

XXX

Words, Words, Words

WHEN hardly thirteen, I was delegated by my father to deliver the Fourth of July declamation in the open-air "bowery" built for the big day. Nature was dilatory in giving me the five feet four inches of my present stature. On that Fourth of July I looked like a child of ten. A thirteen-page prose text had been given me to memorize. Father, being mayor of our metropolis, spoke officially. I had nothing to do but to obey. I may or may not have understood my speech at the time. At any rate, I repeated it over the Wisconsin air without aid of amplification or prompting. This was my debut in public speaking.

As children, we had been given to understand that English was our mother tongue. We were responsible for the correct intelligent use of it. Until 1925 I had no impressive opportunity to demonstrate this ability. That year I spoke to the faculty and students of the graduate department of English at Berkeley. After that followed words, words, words in many places on diverse subjects. One university publication announced that I would appear for a lecture wearing my native costume. The boys wore ties that day. During the flaming twenties I began a talk at a state university convocation with boys and girls in the most casual attitudes. Before the end of the hour they had become attentive young men and women, in posture at least. The Mormons have asked me to talk in the Bishop's house at Salt Lake City, a privilege not often extended to Gentiles, I believe. Quakers have included me in their chapel programs. Mortimer Adler has been in some of my audiences, as I have been in his. The graduate English faculty at Columbia let me talk to them on "Frontiers of Poetry." Helen White was there that evening, and possibly Louise Pound, though I remember her better for her graduate course in Old English. She taught it like first-year Latin, and we learned it.

Through the years there have been innumerable lectures, papers and the like before conventions, confraternities, conferences of Christians and Jews. Recently I have been asked numerous times to talk to non-Catholic groups on meditation, contemplation. Our young people are immensely interested in insight and contemplative thought. They ask honestly how to get into the business of ways and means. I have tried to tell them that contemplation often begins with an earnest consideration of some accepted truth. We take the words apart: *Con-templation* becomes the act or state of being in a temple, perhaps a church, perhaps the out-of-doors, perhaps the mysteries of one's own mind. *Consideration* means being among the stars. Youth needs no more impelling invitation to companionship with God.

Returning by train from Seattle where I had been lecturing not so long ago, I rode for hours through the snow-covered majesty of the high Rockies. Suddenly at one great moment of my life on wheels, I looked out on a fire-scarred skeleton of a giant pine. As I watched, a bald eagle soared into view, moved slowly down, lighted and settled himself majestically on the outstretched arm of the pine. One mountain king in solitude providing a throne for another! In the speeding train I sat awed, wordless, their lone exalted subject.

Something of the making of books of prose has already found place in this chronicle. The volumes, *Chaucer's Nuns and*

Other Essays and *Pearl: A Study in Spiritual Dryness,* both published in 1925, found acceptance in the scholarly world and opened doors to me where I find continued welcome. In 1941 I gathered together manuscripts of lectures and student convocations under the title, *Addressed to Youth.* Our princely Archbishop Cushing paid it the high compliment of saying that he had used every essay in at least one sermon. There are those who can find "sermons in stones, and good in every thing." Beyond these, I have a single prose volume, *A Lost Language and Other Essays,* which came out in 1951. Limits of time have fenced me in sternly. They have determined both the beginnings and ends of the making of books.

They have not prevented what looks to me now, reading the records carefully kept by my long-suffering secretary, a very plethora of monographs, critical essays, articles appearing in magazines on both sides of the Atlantic. Picking names as subjects from among them, I am pleased to find Belloc, Charles Du Bos, Anatole France, Alice Meynell, Francis Thompson, Humbert Wolfe. Does anyone remember him now?

Henry Seidel Canby told me once, "Whatever you may do in critical writing, you will return eventually, I think, to poetry." So far as I have had time for any writing it has been verse. Mr. Canby foresaw the kind but not the conditions of my traffic with words.

Poetry I think of as a distillation requiring undistracted time in large quantities. This no sister that I know of has ever had. What one doesn't have one must make, naturally or supernaturally. The religious life is the model school in resourcefulness. Increasingly, after exchanging manuscript-verse with Father Charles O'Donnell and Joyce Kilmer, I found myself isolating thoughts, husbanding moments walking to and from class, holding every fraction of quiet for milling these thoughts into lyric form. The process has been continuous and almost more secret than my conscience.

Miss Conway often quoted to me the counsel of Saint Jean Baptist de La Salle, "A good work divulged before its time is half destroyed." The acorn keeps the secret of the oak, the bud of the blossom. Even the mother does not know the whole secret of the child within her womb. Nothing is more deadly to creative work than premature exposure. For years, even my closest friends did not dream that I wrote or cared to write anything more important than my letters home.

Meanwhile, I lived with the mental restlessness of wanting to write, the inner nauseas of the half-finished, the great releases of the completed poem. One lyric, one sonnet would be scarcely a week old before the creative process would begin all over again. Each poem might be the last and each clamored for a successor. The religious rule of silence was my best workshop. By virtue of its prevailing interior quiet I wrote at least one poem a month over a period of fifteen or twenty years, every one of which I sent out at once to earn its living by publication in some magazine. They were good children. They all sold themselves.

Apart from religious silence, illness was my second source of solitude. Subject to heavy bronchial colds, I found myself rather often isolated for two or three blessed days. Immediately, I can say intuitively, I set myself to work at something that I had been ruminating on for a long time, or perhaps something that just popped into my head. Both things can happen. All poets chew cuds. Caedmon, the first English poet whose name is known, was the first Anglo-Saxon to confess it.

Recovery from my cold and a new poem were ordinarily synchronous. Later on, my superiors and friends learned of my poetic therapeutics. They would warn me when trying to catch up on rest or vitality, "Now don't be writing poetry!" Honestly, I believe that endless suppression is much more exhausting than any form of writing of which I have experience. It adds up to this: Having never had time within an always heavy and demanding schedule to do any writing, I have done what I have done chiefly when ill, often in hospitals. On such a time the doctor came in to make the professional inquiry, "How do you feel?" "Fine, Doctor," I answered, "I have written a sonnet." Sonnets had neither temperature nor blood pressure for him. Nevertheless, he assumed interest. "Let's see it," he said. I handed him my sonnet, a good one, I believe, entitled "Details for My Burial."

In the course of thirty years I have published ten books of verse, big and little, most of which now appear in a single volume, *Collected Poems.* Sometimes students ask what books are best to read as helps to writing. With no hesitation at all, I say, "The Bible, the Oxford Dictionary, seed catalogues." This is spoken in parable. Here are the words of God, of man, of nature.

What preparation best enables one to be a poet? The Sixth Beatitude, I think, "Blessed are the clean of heart for they shall see God."

XXXI

Will You Walk into My Parlor?

MANY of my waking, working hours during the past twenty-five years have been spent in a double office on the sunny front of Le Mans Hall, a bit beyond the lobby and the great hall. Just inside the door, on the wall to your right hangs the first degree granted by the college. Entirely hand-drawn, hand-lettered, it witnesses to the conferring of the degree of Bachelor of Letters on Agnes Ewing Brown. This academic testimonial is dated June 16, 1898, and signed by Mother M. Annunciata, President of the Board of Trustees.

A wall of books greets you; mutual friends in alphabetical order: Mortimer Adler, Charles Du Bos, Christopher Fry, Romano Guardini, Conrad Hilton, C. S. Lewis, the Maritains, Mauriac, the Sheeds, Sorokin, the Trapps, Eugenio Zolli, former Chief Rabbi of Rome. Central on the shelves are various versions of the Scriptures, new and old; beside them, quite congruously, I think, my books of birds and wildflowers. The shelf below holds the Great Books, and below them, again in complete congruity, professional volumes on Women in Education, Womanpower, and from the first slight text on fund raising by John Price Jones to the newest word with the printers' ink barely dry on it, a collection on the arts and crafts of financing education. Rare and

lucky are the administrators who have not had to replace, temporarily at least, their communication of the liberal and fine arts
with an apprenticeship in public relations, a communing with
corporations, a treasure hunt in the mazes of American foundations.

Flanking these financial Baedekers are volumes of proceedings,
directories, presidents' reports, corporation reports, files. Let us
not linger unduly over them, though they contain treasures.

Yes, there are other walls to my office. A fine fresco of Mary
Magdalen, done by our Sister Edna, and a good copy of Löchner's
"Madonna of the Rose Garden" hang on one. Beside them sit I at
my desk, hours at a time. A map of the world is under the glass
top. Parts of my own world rest on it, not under glass, to be
administered by my best wisdom, judgment, and experience, but
in all ways, in inept though totally devoted apprenticeship to the
Holy Spirit. Above me Pope Pius XII looks down from a large,
beautiful, autographed photograph. A window frames our front
campus. Our devoted Bishop Pursley in photograph smiles at
His Holiness from the opposite side of the window.

Now come into the second half of my working world. This
room we call humorously an old curiosity shop, a nutshell, a squirrel cage. It serves many purposes. It may be a curiosity shop, with
unsuspected surprises for children; a nutshell (reminiscent of
Francis Thompson) sheltering fertile ideas to be matured, lived
with, shared, and ultimately fruitful and life-giving; a squirrel
cage in which dreams, ideas, possibilities revolve in exhilarating
succession for the mere fun and exercise of thinking or more seriously in hope of some future realization. This office has a north
wall of bookshelves and a fireplace, a south wall of windows, an
east wall of maps: London, Oxford, Paris, large, pictorial, exciting. We enter from a door at the west wall which has a frieze of
warm sepia vertical prints from Chartres: the Christ of the South
portal, a Queen of Juda from the west, the angel become sundial
among them, and all from Etienne Houvet himself.

Follow the four-and-a-half feet of wainscoting around the room. Above it you will meet Giotto, Fra Angelico, Bonfigli, Forli, Botticelli, pages from the old French Romance of the Rose in excellent prints, and two rare icons.

The corners of the room are diverting. A medieval bellows leans beside the bookshelf in one of them. It bears the incised inscription, "Amor vincit omnia." This is a nice supplement to the motto on the medal of Madame Eglantine, in Chaucer. Children like to blow little puffs of air at one another through this antique device. Even better, they enjoy ringing all the bells on the bookshelves: the raucous cowbell from a Vermont farm, elephant bells from India, a slender bell from Viet-Nam. On the doorknob hangs the most melodious of all, a small, rough-cast camel's bell from Nazareth. A large hand-bell serves as doorstop. This is one of the few survivors of the generations of such bells that kept guard at the end of every corridor in the days before electric signals and sounded "the tintinnabulary summons" for all classes and assemblies. Only the very reliable students were delegated to ring these bells.

One window corner houses a family of canes and walking sticks, hiking sticks with nationalities and names of their own. Most of our friends enjoy meeting them: the blackthorn— Brother Thorn—from Ireland, Señor Stick from southernmost Mexico, a red birch Brother Stone from the Wasatch mountains. My favorite, a hawthorn, has a name which I will never tell to anyone. Even should you guess the name, I would not admit it. That is not a mental reservation. It is a part of the name, the only part that I share with you.

In the office of an administrator, such an array of sticks calls for an explanation. Many of us like to walk for the sheer joy of it. Some of us like to supplement human companionship with the kindly support of a stick. So we take our choice from the collection and start out on a quest: hepaticas, adder's tongues, fringed gentians in season. Or we try to catch in flight glimpses of migrat-

ing warblers, of the blue bunting, the towhee, the shyer, more
fugitive of our bird friends. Sometimes we simply take the road
"that leads to God knows where." You see, these hiking sticks
have a pleasant life of it.

In autumn we ask Brother Fire to join us. We may build a
small fire of dry leaves and sticks, invoke the spirit of fire, and
with one match, have a merry blaze to watch and wonder at. The
tragedy comes when we must get back to school. Then we have
to beat Brother Fire to death and be certain he is safely buried
before we leave his grave. All of this recaptures for us, so far as
we can guess, some part of the spirit of everybody's Saint Francis.

A globe revolves upon my broad window sill. The world, you
may think, is too much with me. Would you regard as quite ultra
my wish for a sky map, too? A Buddha sits in contemplation on
the small table in the adjoining corner. This came to me through
the courtesy of some of General MacArthur's men when they
were in Japan. The General had told them to watch for any
vestige among the natives that they might find of Christianity
surviving from the days of Saint Francis Xavier. This Buddha
is the fruit of their mission accomplished. Ostensibly, it is the
conventional object of Oriental veneration. But the head can be
lifted off. Within, one finds a small, perfectly carved figure which
might well be the Good Shepherd, or perhaps Our Lady, standing against an aureole shaped like an olive leaf. This type of halo
in some periods of Japanese art indicated divinity. So, through the
courtesy of a great general and his loyal men, my office becomes a
shrine to a hidden God. And who does not recognize that "the
grace of God is in courtesy"?

As my mother told you long ago, my books are my friends.
Here they are again, shelf upon shelf, the poets from Beowulf
and Langland to Eliot and Millay and Daniel Berrigan on the
left of the fireplace, the mystics on the right. Lead me not into
digression or we shall never emerge from this room.

The fireplace is not so much an altar for burnt offerings as a shrine for the unforgotten and the unforgettable. A large oil portrait of Sister Rita is central in the wall above it. This was sent to us by the secretary of Elizabeth Jordan after Miss Jordan's death. It had hung in her office from the time of Sister's death and was painted from a passport picture, the only photograph Sister ever had taken, I am quite sure. In her day, kodaks were not ubiquitous and the camera had anything but the right of way.

A delicate bisque statue of our Lady, an ancient ivory chalice, and a fine crucifix, enamel on copper, a gift of Clare Luce, share the mantel with Sister.

Chairs? Yes, there are two, upholstered in soft red velvet brocade, fit for an abbess or a prioress, in which I practically never sit. But many guests come to honor them. Four sturdy Windsor chairs serve workaday purposes and gather confreres around the table. Here many fascinating issues come to life, or are led to execution (an ambiguous statement; interpret it as you like!). You should know that under this glass table top a reproduction of a medieval almanac from an old copy of *L'Illustration* spreads out before us the months of the year, the signs of the zodiac, creation, the tree of life, Adam and Eve sharing their mortal repast, and the Nativity. Although we have been contemplating this triple panorama for years it preserves, like the very world it portrays, a perennial charm.

Many current problems in education Bishop Edwin O'Hara has brought to this table, he, however, properly seated in the crimson brocade chair. Years ago we spoke of the two absolute impediments to receiving Holy Communion: mortal sin and food and drink. I regretted that their innocent little breakfasts prevented thousands of children from going to Holy Communion as they assisted at daily Mass before school. His Excellency urged the matter of reverence. Happily, our Holy Father has established the perfect solution.

Father Vincent Donovan, O.P., has shared here our problems

on the chanting of the Office and set our feet on the first steps toward improvement.

Before beginning his active crusade for Mary, Father Peyton came here with his great dream, the rosary recited in tens of thousands of American homes. We talked of ways and means. We had friends in Hollywood who proved helpful. Later, Father returned to my office with a greater dream, that of the air, the world of radio. Here I was helpless. "But I will send you to someone who can help you, Father," I said, and gave him the name, telephone number and address of Mr. William E. Cotter. Bill Cotter, one of Notre Dame's devoted sons, was at the time counsel for the Union Carbide Company in New York City. I wrote him and his wife Evarista, saying, "I am sending you a saint. Do whatever he asks you." Obediently, Bill took Father Peyton to the president of the Mutual Broadcasting Company. The nation-wide broadcast of the Joyful, Sorrowful, and Glorious hours resulted inevitably. Who can resist Father Peyton?

Some years ago we entertained Father Arrupe here, the Jesuit Doctor who stood with the Master of Novices on the hill outside the novitiate overlooking Hiroshima that morning in 1945 which most Americans, I believe, wish might be undone. Without knowing what had happened, the two priests found themselves face downward on the ground. Rising from their daze and prostration, they looked out to where the city had been, to see practical annihilation. Within the half hour people came running to the Doctor Jesuit for help, mouths bleeding, skin burned beyond healing, death overtaking them from no apparent cause.

In 1946, a young Jesuit, Father Eric Paul Hilsdale presented to Father Arrupe the chalice used at his first Mass and made by special permission from uranium, cobalt, silver, gold. It has been called the Atomic Chalice and was sent to Hiroshima in reparation and in petition that the elements contained in it would "never be profaned by man's hatred of man and exploded in the face of defenseless humanity." This is Father Hilsdale's prayer.

Other friends from the Orient share my nutshell, my office, my table. A fortnight ago our two Carmelite nuns from Madras, India, brought in jars of ginger, cloves, black pepper, allspice grown in their own native gardens. Two black ivory elephants, an ebony lion, lacquered boxes from Burma come from other Oriental sisters in our household.

Stalwart girls from Ghana, sensitive students from Uganda, youth from all the world walk into this parlor of mine, sometimes with parents and problems, always with the promise, with the possibilities of youth. To these I am completely captive.

You realize that these are just parts for the whole, the briefest briefs for "all God's chillun" who cross my threshold. You may have been among them more than once. If so, I remember.

This one beautiful group you must meet. A family of five came to leave the eldest daughter at our novitiate. As they said good-bye, the father stepped back to be last in leaving the room. Boyishly young in appearance, he said to me as only a father can, "Take care of her, Sister." What a valedictory!

This has been a long detour to my inner office. I have not meant to tire you. My invitation to walk into my parlor is sincere. That is a day without salt, indeed, that does not bring the ends of the earth together in this small world of mine. Someday it may bring you.

XXXII

An Old Lady Shows Her Medals

SINCE I was six years old I have been in school all my life. From my nineteenth year, I have lived under the same roof with high school and college girls: teaching them, breaking bread with them, playing with them, praying with them. They are a goodly company of little sisters. Many of them, I am sure, had not, when I knew them, lost their baptismal innocence. Most of them at all times were, I pray God, in the state of sanctifying grace. You see how skyscraping an experience would have been that of taking off our bodies and sitting in our souls.

I have had great teachers. Mother Pauline, as president of Saint Mary's College, first put me in graduate school at the University of Notre Dame where I earned my Master's degree in 1918. Sister Celsus, my superior in Ogden, and Mother Barbara in Woodland, California, saw to it that I completed my work for my doctorate at the University of California. Mother Vincentia, our superior general, sent me to Europe with a focus on Oxford in 1933 and 1934.

Elizabeth Havican entered Saint Mary's College in 1911. In 1918 I dressed her in the Holy Habit. As Mother Rose Elizabeth, our superior general, she believed in me, bore patiently with me for twelve years. In 1937 I asked that Sister Kathryn Marie, a teacher at Holy Cross Academy, Washington, be transferred from her eastern province to Saint Mary's as our dean of women. The request was granted. In turn dean, superior, Midwestern provincial, Mother Kathryn Marie, now our superior general, forbears while I explain to her all the reasons for letting me do what I wish.

At the end of fifty active years, spent on many missions in a large community, I think back, look back with gratitude and love on all my sisters, so patient in bearing with me, so generous in helping me, so kind in forgetting my failures. Enumeration being impossible, I include you all in this my grateful memento for the living.

Great teachers have been matched with great friends. Always they have come into my life when I have most needed them. Last year I traveled through the West with a young sister. One bishop, one priest after another we met whom I had known as little boys. Explaining the informality of our conversation, I would say to Sister, "I knew him when he was in knee pants." Commenting on our trip after our return, I asked her if I had worn her out. "Not quite," she said, "but I have yet to meet a bishop whom I knew in knee pants."

Looking back over the years on mission and at Saint Mary's, I find them set against a background of crimson and purple, black and white. The Church speaks a dignified language. Your Eminence, Your Excellency lift us up to the splendor of our family and its care for us. Cardinal Stritch, now with God, is more than ever our patron. Cardinal Spellman we claim as an honorary alumnus. Bishop Pursley meets our every need, distinguishes our world in his kindly solicitude. "Father" is the basic word for them all. I have known, cherished, been directed by their goodness, wisdom, holiness. God has sent these friends to me, or me to them in the needs which only they could meet. They are a part of the "divine assistance" for which we ask earnestly at the end of every meal. Occasionally, when something particularly desirable had taken place, our superior used to say, "How did that happen?" "We ask for the divine assistance every day, Mother," I would answer, "and we get it."

Sixteen years ago a beautiful, gifted young English girl came to New York at the invitation of the International Federation of Catholic Alumnae. A wire from Marion McCandless, our alumnae secretary attending the meeting, urged me to invite this remarkable Barbara Ward to Saint Mary's. She came, talked amazingly to us, stayed overnight with us. Last spring she came back, though in memory we had never let her leave us. Now as Lady Barbara Jackson, former editor of the *Economist*, visiting professor at Harvard, she returns to us, her Saint Mary's family, as to the home of her spirit, to a world that loves her deeply.

For the commencement commemorating our centenary we invited Clare Boothe Luce to be our speaker. From piles of invitations, she asked Bishop Sheen which to accept. "Go to Sister Madeleva," he said. She came for that first magical visit to us. Her name is a brightness, a light so right for her. "Clare" and "Luce" are both words for the luminous elation which to me is so much herself. Mr. Luce came, too, last June at Notre Dame's conferring of the Laetare Medal on her. As we sat in the guest dining room, eating raisin toast with tea before their flight back to New York, we knew, in their essence, the fine amenities of friendship. Recently, Louisa Jenkins has joined them. What a meeting of great minds!

More than once in years past Sir Arnold Lunn has landed literally on our threshold in an almost nonstop flight from Chile. A day or a fortnight here always meant groups of students in heated controversy with this past master in debate.

The visits of Jacques Maritain, his wife Raïssa, her sister Vera have brought with them the tranquillity of order proper to our best-loved philosopher, the palpable peace of our dear, near-saint. Charles De Koninck in his biennial sojourns at Saint Mary's challenges our mentalities, our philosophic training for every bit of all that they are worth.

Helen Iswolsky came to us to complete her second book on Russia, *Light Before Dusk*. Jean Charlot built himself into our world in fifteen great frescoes representing the fine arts in Moreau Hall. The Trapp family have been our house guests more than once to sing not only their unique concerts but Mass and Benediction as well. Baroness Elizabeth Guttenberg has brought us her heroic apostolate and a share in the mystery of Theresa Neumann, her close friend.

Year after year, with intervals of interruption, Robert Speaight comes to us as a guest-professor. He brings the poetry of Gerard Manley Hopkins, T. S. Eliot, the contemporary poetic drama of Christopher Fry, the great Belloc and, more than all, Shakespeare. His productions with student casts of *A Midsummer Night's Dream* and *Twelfth Night* will continue to be major achievements in the life of the college. Through Mr. Speaight, Martin Browne and his wife have revived at Saint Mary's the great half-forgotten text of the old York cycle mystery plays from the Creation to General Judgment.

In a staff of well over a hundred teachers, more than half are excellent lay faculty members, each bringing to the college his or her own capacities to dream for it, to work toward the realization of their dreams. I have in mind the Moreau Quartet, our debating team which ranks seventh among forty-seven national teams, and which won from the Army, the second-best team in the country this year. I have in mind the designs of Norman Laliberte, rated among the best designers in America. I have in mind our upper division Christian Culture course, resting on Christopher Dawson's theory of philosophy of education and directed by Dr. Bruno Schlesinger. But why enumerate? I have in mind every member of the faculty who according to the fullness of preparation and generosity of spirit is building Saint Mary's into a college worthy of its past, prophetic of its future. I have in mind the great corporations that are making history of their benefactions to our private colleges: the Ford Foundation, United States Steel, Esso, Sears and Roebuck and their com-

panions. How many of us wear the Maecenas medals for them?
Within our own state of Indiana, companionships established by
our Conference on Higher Education and our Conference of
Church-related Colleges are dear to me personally and invaluable
professionally. The Lilly Foundation has given us memorable in-
centive and help. Mr. Pattillo's interpretations of these have been
experiences in gracious encouragement for which we are grateful.

I leave the campus for the moment. Because of their absolute
generosity and kindness to me, I call the Lahey Clinic and Dr.
John Norcross my medal of Hippocrates. They have made life
physically very worth living.

I have a group of Holy Innocents medals that I want to show
you: the children who play with the trinkets in my office, who
ring all my many bells, the little boys who carry off my hiking
sticks, the little girls who want to try on my cap. Then come the
boys and girls who write to me during Book Month or when preparing their long composition about some living author, or when
taking my name in confirmation. Every one of these letters I
answer personally. For twenty years one such correspondence has
lasted—with Geraldine Madeleva Strouse. One specimen letter
from another Holy Innocent must stand for all:

> Dear Sr. Mary Madeleva,
>
> In our literature class last week we juniors had to draw a
> famous writer's name from one of the freshmen's green and
> white uniform hats that was floating around that day. I was
> lucky. I drew your lovely name which is very much cher-
> ished here at Saint Gertrude's. I think it suits your very
> attractive and overly friendly face which I studied when I
> looked up your well-spent life in the only books which
> should be honored to have your poem on the pages. Namely
> The Scholastic and the Catholic Authors Books.
>
> I am writing to ask if you would mind very much to give
> me in 400 words incidents or happenings in your life which

are not in these books. You see we have to have 2,000 words in by December 22, and I have gotten 1,600, which is good considering that you are still living.

Hoping this won't inconvenience you,

Sincerely,
Barbara Kelly

I like to tell our students that they are not complete Saint Mary's women until they are graduated, alumnae; until then they are only in the process.

In 1950 I asked Marion McCandless to write a history of the alumnae. In April, 1952, *Family Portraits* was off the press, a compendium of my college family. Most of them are acquainted with me or I with them only on paper. But in the expansiveness of the Saint Mary's life and the Holy Cross spirit we all love one another. For half my life Marion has been a composite of our Saint Mary's world. In putting her last among my best friends, my Saint Mary's medals, I am including every Saint Mary's girl whose name she knows, or does not know—if any there be. I am including her most of all. I am putting my arms figuratively around Marion in an attempt to expand my capacities for love and loyalty, somehow to approximate hers.

One rotund Hoosier medal I prize for President Herman G. Wells who bravely invited me into the alumnae family of our state university.

Two medals in one I have kept for all but last: the Laetare and the Lady of the Holy Sepulcher. Irene Dunne wears both of them. In May she came with her friend and our alumna, Nurma Waite Huesman, to give our commencement address and to receive our Honorary Degree in Letters. Speaking on "A Lamp at the Door" she lighted the way to all great womanhood through the shining example of her own.

As you have already noticed, no chronological order has been imposed upon this display. Nor would I know how to achieve such order. A certain congruity is all that I can pretend to. By virtue of that I show these last very special medals. Some years ago one of our students asked me to walk out on the campus with her. A few days earlier I had helped her with a letter of application to a Carmelite novitiate. So to begin conversation, I asked,

"Alberta, what do you think is the most important thing in the world?"

Without a breath of hesitation and with absolute conviction, she replied, "Sister, I think love is."

She was the last girl in the college to romanticize on anything. As we continued our walk, I asked again, "How do you pray?"

At this, she stopped for a bit, then answered, "By conversation mostly now, I think."

This I submit as one of the great experiences of my life. Alberta is my Carmelite medal.

Within the past few years I have had the privilege of reading in manuscript the poems and plays of Sister Francis, P.C., and of assisting in some small way the writing of this very gifted young nun. She is my Poor Clare medal.

A decade ago one of our graduates in classics entered our graduate School of Sacred Theology. Four years later, as a Doctor of Philosophy, she became a member of our college faculty in the department of Theology. Today she is a professed cloistered Dominican in the Monastery of Our Lady of Grace, North Guilford, Connecticut. As Sister Mary of God, she is our beloved Holy Cross medal of Saint Dominic.

Two names are met here under the aegis of the Order of Preachers and the contemplative life: Father Raymond Bruckberger and Father Louis (Thomas Merton). Father Bruckberger, long a friend through the printed page, has come to us happily this year as a guest and a personal friend. We have shared his rare and penetrating insights into the infinite drama of sanctity and the cast of humanity playing each an indispensable role in that drama.

Among the first students in our School of Sacred Theology was a young woman directed to Saint Mary's by the (then) Dom Verner Moore. She became most interested in Father Louis (Thomas Merton) whose poems I had given her. Of her own initiative she wrote to Father Louis at the Trappist Monastery, Gethsemani, asking him for an explanation of contemplation. His generous answer came in manuscript, entitled "What Is Contemplation?" with permission to publish it at Saint Mary's if we wished. So through the great and simple charity of Father Louis and his superior we have had the privilege of publishing the first prose essay of what has become an elite library of Trappist spirituality.

These are my medals. I show them proudly. There are others. These I speak of gratefully and humbly in recognition of the generous groups who chose me as recipients: The Poet's Corner Award, the National Poetry Award of the New York World's Fair, the Siena Medal, the Woman of Achievement Award.

Having saved the very best for the last, let me register myself a grateful, happy honorary alumna of Mount Mary College, Manhattan College, the University of Notre Dame, Manhattanville College of the Sacred Heart, the University of Indiana. The old lady has showed her medals.

XXXIII

Have I Forgotten Anything?

HAVE I forgotten anything? Through the fallibilities of memory, most probably I have. But, in intention and in the very depths of being, I have not. Nothing that has entered into or touched these seventy years of my lived life has been unrecorded. My present self contains the complete archives, with nothing omitted or deleted. Caring for all, cherishing every contributing factor to a total self, I must bear witness to memory, must acquit my debts with a "thank you" for every contribution.

They include gracious days with Margaret Anglin, quick-charged hours, hours on tiptoe, I thought, with Judith Anderson at Saint Mary's, an afternoon at his California home with Robinson Jeffers, the kindliness of Leo McCarey in the West and at home, the treasure hunt with Ketti Frings and her sister at Saint Mary's. How can I recapture our day as hostess to Sigrid Undset in Chicago, the somber undercurrents in all her profound speech with its typical Nordic falling inflections, her sense of the ominous pervading even the ovation of her truly American welcome. We invited her to come to Saint Mary's to be an author in residence for the duration of war. The peace of our world, however, took her too far from the Atlantic seaboard where her contacts with her children in Europe were more immediate.

Bruce Marshall must have a paragraph of his own, whether as guest at Saint Mary's, at our Paris convent home on Rue de Vaugirard or at his home with his lovely wife and daughter. Although this Josephine has now grown to womanhood, I still cherish her as the dear bilingual baby that I knew.

How shall I commit Evelyn Waugh and his wife to the limits of a paragraph? Fortunately, memory transcends the strictures of words, preserving for us the companionship of dinner and a rare evening together. I like to remember the roll call of the absent Waugh children that, for all its British detachment, brought these thriving sons and daughters into our Saint Mary's family circle.

Sir Shane Leslie, sometime in kilts, but always in a multitude of irrepressible and unpredictable capacities, is not one but many memories. These every student who knew him in his scholarly lectures or in his facetious moments will not forget.

In the middle thirties, members of the faculty of Saint Mary's and Notre Dame gravitated to a center of mutual interests—the writing of verse. They called themselves the Holy Rood Poetry Society, met once a month at Saint Mary's, submitting at each meeting unsigned copies of such original work as they wished to go through the clinic of criticism and to run the gantlet of the devil's advocate. Norbert Engels often filled this office with the humor and efficiency that dealt death to doggerel. Louis and Lucille Hasley, John Nims, Henry Rago, Rufus Rauch, Robert Speaight still constitute a solid core of poets and appraisers of poetry among us.

Neither our faculty nor I have forgotten our series of conferences by the scholarly Praemonstratensian, Father Gabriel, on medieval education and the philosopher, Joseph Pieper, on the intellectual virtues. An afternoon that Dom Virgil Michael, O.S.B., and Mortimer Adler spent with us in the early days of the Great Books program is a poignant memory. As we disbanded, we watched the two young philosophers walk down the hall like two splendid boys. They were scarcely older than that. Two weeks later Father Virgil had gone to God.

Out of our friendship with Mr. Adler and Scott Buchanan came an invitation to lecture to the students at Saint John's College, Annapolis. There were my talk and a longer discussion after the talk and hours on the terrace at the home of President Stringfellow Barr, trying to find our way through the four last things. Immortality can be almost as endless in discussion as in reality. Do you remember, Dr. Barr?

Other audiences of college boys I recall. Chief among them are the graduates at Saint John's College, Minnesota, and at Saint Mary's College, California, to whom I had the privilege of giving commencement addresses.

The Seventy-fifth Anniversary of Manhattan College brought me to that campus for an unforgettable commencement. On the stage with the officers of administration were Cardinal Hayes, Father Robert Gannon, S.J., Alexis Carrel. Father Gannon was the brilliant, witty chronicler for the Christian Brothers as Christian educators in repartee with the Sons of Saint Ignatius in the same role. To those of us present, the experience was one of unforgettable intellectual delectation.

In 1957 another equally memorable son of Saint Ignatius brought his gifts of wisdom and wit to Saint Mary's College for our commencement, Father Joseph Christie of Farm Street, London. Early in that scholastic year he had directed the exercises of the annual retreat for the students, preparing the seniors, at least, for the sequel of graduation.

No, I have not forgotten our hours of driving north to the very dubious trickle of water in the wilderness, the source of the Mississippi river, or our hours of driving over difficult roads in a difficult car, across miles of one of the many mouths of the Mississippi to New Orleans. I have not forgotten weeks at Land-O'Lakes, our frightening a fawn from its protective-colored nest and my helpless anxiety for this little Bambi and its mother. I have not forgotten our trips to Georgian Bay, down the Saint Lawrence and up the Saguenay, our weeks at Stratford, Ontario, for the Shakespearean Festival, and our good friends, Tom Flood and Tom Patterson.

The hearts and homes that you have opened to me at Harts-dale, Beekman Place, New York, Golden Beach, Miami, Joliet, Fort Wayne, Tulsa, Laramie, Los Angeles, San Diego: these I have not forgotten.

There are those who remembered with me books planned to-gether, books collaborated on, galley proofs read and manuscripts mended. Maurice Lavanoux recalls with me that he gave his first lecture at Saint Mary's. *Spirit* and *Jubilee* have given me place in their planning. Mr. E. I. Watkin may remember his manuscript still with me and my wildflower books in England with him. Anne Fremantle and Alice Curtayne are still with us in the charm of memory. Never shall I forget the midnight during Christmas holiday when our good stewardess, Sister Adela, came to my door apologizing, "I am sorry to wake you, but the fifth floor is on fire." Someone had left an electric iron on. By four in the morning, the fire was out, the water mopped up, all roofs still over our heads, the firemen regaled with coffee and doughnuts; all except the fire chief. He did not break his fast. He was going to Holy Communion in the morning. How happily our present dispensation would have served him that strenuous night.

I am by no means forgetting the education of Sister Madeleva, my induction into fund-raising by the John Price Jones Com-pany, first by Mr. Jones himself, now in process under the direc-tion of Charlie Anger and his henchmen, Bob Johnston and Peter Wolkodoff. Apropos of this business of financing education in one's own college, who that attended can forget the Saint Pat-rick's day brunch in Oakland where I spoke to two hundred Christians and Jews, each with a sprig of fresh shamrock flown in from Ireland that morning!

I have a board of trustees, bounded only by the United States;

a generous President's Council, inspired by Lincoln Sollitt and never to be forgotten by me.

Saint Mary's and I have our providentially built-in relationship, our big brother family bond with the University of Notre Dame, never more generously realized than in its esteemed superior general, Father O'Toole, its always available procurator, Father Heston (a native son of South Bend), its kindly provincial, Father Mehling, and its priestly teacher-president, everybody's Father Hesburgh.

In virtue of belonging to this Holy Cross family I found myself standing in line with university and corporation presidents in the lobby of the administration building of the University of Notre Dame one September morning in 1952, shaking hands with President-to-be Eisenhower and "Mamie" on their brief visit to South Bend. By the same token we greeted Vice-President Nixon and his wife some years later.

The University has brought to our world the genius of our great Mestrovich and his devoted wife and children. Their families are now our families as well.

Why is it so easy to expect one's friends to understand? Because I could not call the roll of all, I have not mentioned many of you by name. But I have kept this last best place for you. Because you are friends, you do understand. You do take your place, each of you, in these my seventy years. I know that you have not forgotten. You must believe that I remember with gratitude and love.

XXXIV

The Relaxed Grasp

BEFORE I was in the novitiate four months the only sister who had counseled me in any way regarding the religious life was sent on mission. I never saw her again. Sister Rita, my dream lady, died just a month before I left the novitiate. I never had a day's opportunity of knowing her simply as a sister-friend. By these two tokens and even then I understood that God meant me to live without props. He was making my natural independence an asset rather than an obstacle. My friendships rested on mutual interests, enthusiasms, objectives. I had to do my own thinking, make my own decisions, with proper deference to others. This gives one a capacity to be alone. Sometimes it almost imposes aloneness on one. There are compensations.

When I was a very young sister I came upon an essay by Louise Imogene Guiney, entitled "La Sainte Indifférente." I found just what I needed and at the exact moment of my need. Let me quote the paragraphs which have dominated my life, this description of the saint of holy indifference:

> "Of all his store, unconsciously increased, he can always part with sixteen-seventeenths, by way of concessions to his individuality, and think the subtraction so much concealing marble chipped from the heroic figure of himself. . . .

"He has gone through volition, and come out at the other side of it; everything with him is a specific act: he has no habits.

"Nothing is so vulgar as close suction. He will never tighten his fingers on loaned opportunity; he is a gentleman, the hero of the habitually relaxed grasp."

When I left Saint Mary's, my school and convent home for thirteen years, I loosed my hold on friends, pupils, places, things. I went to a world of missionary possibilities, of compensatory rich friendships, of the majesty of the mountains, a new world of birds and wildflowers. It was a life one spent on tiptoe, at least for me.

Three years later it was exchanged for California spring in February, a world rose-filled in April, and exotic summers until the winter rains. Then I watched the orange and other citrus fruits hanging heavy on the trees bleach rather than ripen. The Pacific gave itself to me down all the miles of its matchless coast. The trees, from pepper to redwood, were mine, the purple finches, the mockingbirds.

Better, there were the colleges that I knew, some before they were born, some in their robust youth, all in their beautiful promise and fulfillment. I think of Dominican College of San Rafael, which I knew when its enrollment numbered five students, two of whom were sisters. I was studying with the Sisters of Notre Dame de Namur when they pulled themselves up by the roots in San Jose and moved to Belmont. This was a major lesson in the relaxed grasp. I spoke to the first students at Mount Saint Mary's College, Los Angeles, when I had to step on a box to enter the only accessible door of the first building then under construction. I remember watching the fog roll over twin peaks in San Francisco long before the College of San Francisco transfigured that great eminence. Best of all, new worlds of the mind and of the soul opened in California, with new friends to stimulate and to share them. These, too, must teach me the relaxed grasp. These, too, I left to return to the work of building a college on a mountainside. Of this I have already spoken.

I did not mention that living among the mountains involves mountain climbing. This calls for hiking sticks. When I left Saint Mary-of-the-Wasatch I had in my office a collection of hand-picked, carved and polished hiking sticks that had journeyed miles with me to the tops of all our surrounding mountains and back. They had shared our quest of wildflowers: fritillary, lupine, lungwort, pentstemon, cliff rose, columbine. They had shared with us the first call of the meadow lark, the iridescence of the lazuli bunting, the splendor of the western oriole. They were friends to leave behind.

On returning to Saint Mary's after fifteen years I did not have enough to fill one small trunk. This is at least an outward sign of the emancipation achieved by the relaxed grasp.

For twenty-five years I have occupied an outer and an inner office in Le Mans Hall at Saint Mary's. Either could be mistaken for an old curiosity shop. A half-dozen or more hiking sticks make a curious collection in the corner of the inner office. Some day I may put them as a holocaust on the roaring fire in our Great Hall, a perfect burnt offering. But not yet!

When, before dawn, on August 15 of last year, God came for Bill Cotter, the realization left me bereaved as no other death could have. The relaxed grasp—how could I translate it into comfort for Evarista, his sweetheart-wife, my schoolmate-friend? When a fortnight later Helen Holland Voll died, my grasp relaxed on a second of my lifetime and most dear friends. On Thanksgiving Day the astounding word came that John O'Laughlin, after a day in his office working in apparent health, had died before all of his family could reach him. I began to understand that God was taking me in earnest. He loves these friends of mine even better than I do. I am learning to let go in deference to Him.

A little Chinese sister came to study with us some time ago. She had seen her family shattered, her young religious community dispersed. Her entire world, materially, consisted of two small suitcases, filled with absolutely essential clothing. She understood little English and spoke less. During our annual retreat which she was trying to make with us I thought to help her by talking over with her slowly and simply the matter of each conference. After the instruction on poverty, I asked, "Sister, did you understand Father's talk?" "He talk on poverty," she answered; then added, "Sister, you come to my room." We went upstairs together. She opened her suitcases, put their entire contents out on the bed, everything, I believe, except her toothbrush and soap. "Now, Sister," she said, "you take what I do not need." Here was an Oriental girl of twenty-five, a refugee, alone in every possible way, understanding and practicing as I had never had to do the absolutes of detachment, of holy poverty. What had my years taught me of the relaxed grasp?

I am, however, en route. I like to go to Marshall Field's in Chicago just to see how many things there are in the world that I do not want. There have been, still are, books that I should like at least to try to write, cuds of song upon which I still hope to chew. I should like to watch my seedling oaks and beeches grow into great trees. Thinking of things to be done, hopes to be realized, persons to be helped, I say laughingly that I go to a multitude of funerals daily, burying so many deceased projects, so much of what I have had to let die and must bury without regret. Some day I shall have only One, Infinite, Absolute want. I shall not even want, for the time being, my body. I shall not even want the breath I breathe. When the last nonessentials of encumbering humanity have been cut away, when the last tenacious grasp has been relaxed, what shall I say? What shall I say when I see God?